United States Department of Agriculture

I0484885

Economic
Research
Service

Situation and
Outlook

SSS-M-310

June 18, 2014

Sugar and Sweeteners Outlook

Stephen Haley, coordinator
shaley@ers.usda.gov

NAFTA Sugar June 2014

The next release is
July 17, 2014

Approved by the
World Agricultural
Outlook Board.

The Mexico 2013/14 forecast for sugar production is lowered from last month by 250,000 metric tons (MT) to 6.10 million MT as output continues to lag well behind last year's pace. Given lower supplies and sharply higher domestic prices, total exports are reduced by 121,000 MT to 2.278 million. However, exports to the United States are raised based on the pace to date, and exports to the rest of the world are forecast lower. Ending stocks fall by 129,000 MT to 818,000 MT, or 19.0 percent of consumption. For 2014/15, beginning stocks and exports are forecast lower. However, relatively higher prices in the U.S. sugar market provide the incentive for increased 2014/15 exports to the United States.

Total 2013/14 U.S. supply is forecast to rise by 261,000 short tons, raw value (STRV), with a 10,000 STRV increase in sugar from sugarcane production in Texas and a 251,000 STRV increase in imports. Imports under the re-export program are raised 100,000 STRV, based on industry estimates, and imports from Mexico are increased 151,000 STRV. With total use unchanged, ending stocks are forecast to rise to 15.0 percent of use, compared with 12.9 percent in May.

Recent *Sugar and Sweeteners Outlook* Special Articles

"Long-term Projection of U.S. and Mexico Sugar Supply and Use through 2024/25," pdf pages 3-17 of the *Sugar and Sweetener* report (http://www.ers.usda.gov/publications/sssm-sugar-and-sweeteners-outlook/sssm306.aspx).

"The Road to Forfeitures," pdf pages 12-17 of the *Sugar and Sweetener* report http://www.ers.usda.gov/publications/sssm-sugar-and-sweeteners-outlook/sssm303.aspx).

Total 2014/15 U.S. supply is projected up 811,000 STRV, with increases in beginning stocks and imports more than offsetting reduced production. Beginning stocks, at 1.857 million STRV, are up 261,000 STRV. Total sugar production is lowered 140,000 STRV, due to lower sugarcane production in Florida and Louisiana based on processors' first projections for 2014/15. Total imports are forecast 690,000 STRV above May due to increased shipments from Mexico. With no changes in total use, ending stocks are forecast to rise to 15.8 percent of 2014/15 use from 9.1 percent.

World Sugar

On May 22, 2014, the U.S. Department of Agriculture (USDA) released the World Production, Supply, and Distribution (PSD) for centrifugal sugar. Included in the May 2014 sugar PSD were new supply and use estimates for the 2013/14 marketing year, first projections of supply and use for 2014/15, and some revisions to older data. The USDA bases most of its estimates and projections on information contained in various Sugar Annuals published through the Global Agricultural Information Network (GAIN) of USDA's Foreign Agricultural Service (FAS).[1]

Table A-1 in the appendix shows supply sources (beginning stocks, production, and imports) and use (exports, domestic consumption, and ending stocks) for major countries and aggregate regions. World exports are projected in 2014/15 to be at about the same level as in 2013/14, or 55.24 million metric tons raw value (MTRV). Exports from Brazil in 2014/15 are expected at 25.250 million MTRV, a reduction of about 3.6 percent from 2013/14.

The USDA forecasts Brazil Center/South sugarcane production at 575 million mt, 3.5 percent lower than last year, and production in the North/Northeast at 54 million mt, about the same as last year. Center/South production prospects have been negatively affected by drought and below-average replanting. The level of total reducing sugars (TRS) has also been affected by the weather, as well as diminished by increased reliance on higher mechanization in harvesting, and has been now forecast 131.5 kilograms, 2 kilograms lower than in 2013/14. The USDA projects that the percentage of TRS going to sugar will increase to 46.5 percent, up from 45.5 percent in 2013/14. Because hydrous ethanol has lost much of its competitive strength to gasoline, whose price is set lower than equilibrium by the Brazilian Government, sugar production is favored and the resulting ethanol production is more for anhydrous ethanol blended with gasoline. All in all, 2014/15 sugar production is forecast at 36.8 million MTRV, down 1 percent nationally. Domestic consumption is forecast to increase by 240,000 MTRV due to population growth and increased demand by food processors. Because stockholding is insignificant, exports balance out supply and demand. Raw sugar should account for 20.2 million MTRV, with the remainder exported as refined sugar.

With the publication of the sugar PSD, the USDA noted the following developments in other sugar producing and trading countries:

Thailand: The USDA projects sugar production will decline 400,000 MTRV to 11.0 million MTRV as sugarcane yields return to normal, more than offsetting an increase in area. Consumption continues to trend higher, driven by rising household and industrial use. Exports are forecast to jump to a record 8.3 million MTRV based on growing Asian demand, particularly from Indonesia and Cambodia. Exports will likely benefit from the Association of Southeast Asian Nations Economic Community Agreement.

Australia: The USDA projects Australian 2014/15 sugar production slightly higher at 4.4 million MTRV due to improved yields, better rainfall, higher dam-storage levels in sugarcane regions, and an easing of drought conditions. Australian sugar exports are projected at 3.1 million MTRV in 2014/15, slightly higher than in the previous 2 years. Access to Korea, Australia's largest market, was increased under a free trade agreement in April 2014.

Guatemala: The USDA projects Guatemalan sugar production for 2014/15 at 2.9 million MTRV, the same as the record high in 2013/14. Total exports for 2014/15 are forecast at 2.0 million MTRV. The Guatemalan sugar industry continues to be one of the most efficient in productivity and port loading capacity (2,200 MT/hour). Guatemala has the largest storage capacity in the Central American region (431,000 MT).

India: The USDA forecasts sugar production to increase nearly 900,000 MTRV to 27.9 million MTRV due to higher yields. With consumption expected to continue its strong rise, exports are forecast to fall to 1.5 million MTRV to meet domestic demand.

Pakistan: The USDA forecasts 2014/15 sugar production at 4.86 million tons, a 7.0 percent decrease from the current-year production estimate. Sugar consumption for 2014/15 is forecast at 4.5 million MTRV, slightly higher

---

[1] http://gain.fas.usda.gov/Lists/Advanced%20Search/AllItems.aspx.

than last year's estimate, and exports are forecast at 400,000 MTRV. Ending stocks are expected to increase to 1.14 million MTRV. The USDA revised the 2013/14 production estimate up 245,000 MTRV to a record 5.2 million MTRV, attributable to increased acreage, good rains, and an improvement in sugar recovery rate.

European Union: The USDA forecasts production at 16.3 million MTRV, up 200,000 MTRV based on both increased sugarbeet area and yield. As consumption continues to trend higher, imports are forecast to grow by 250,000 MTRV to 3.8 million MTRV. Exports remain at 1.5 million MTRV, limited by the sugar export ceiling in the World Trade Organization.

China: The USDA forecasts production at 13.7 million MTRV, down 600,000 MTRV based on lower expected crop yields. Rising consumption, which outpaces production, and lower imports are expected to draw down stocks.

Russia: The USDA forecasts steady production at 4.4 million MTRV. An increase in area is offset by reduced yield. Consumption and imports are forecast down slightly.

South Africa: The USDA forecasts 2014/15 sugar production at 2.5 million MTRV, 3.0 percent higher than in 2013/14. With the expectation of sufficient sugar stocks at the end of the year, exports are projected to total about 1.0 million MTRV of sugar in 2014/15. Sugar imports are expected to decline to about 250,000 MTRV in 2014/15, due to an expected increase in the sugar import tariff.

Swaziland: The USDA forecasts 2014/15 production at 725,000 MTRV, based on a 6.0 percent increase in sugarcane production stemming from increases in area. Exports, mainly to the European Union, are expected to increase by about 3.0 percent to 385,000 MTRV. In 2013/14, sugar production had increased by 3.0 percent from the previous year to an estimated 679,934 MTRV.

Trends in World Sugar Supply and Use

Figure 1 shows year-over-year changes in world sugar supply and use components for 2014/15. Most changes from 2013/14 are relatively minor. The largest change predicted by USDA is growth in world sugar consumption by over 2.5 million MTRV. World production is shown lower, while expansion in consumption drew down the stocks built up from the previous 2 years.

Figure 2 shows world sugar production, consumption, and ending stocks from 2000/01 through a projected 2014/15. Figure 3 focuses on the changes in the world sugar surplus/deficit measure (total production less total use) and ending stocks-to-consumption ratios since 2007/08. Both figures show world production surpluses since 2010/11 and the strong buildup of stocks starting in 2010/11 and reaching their maximum level in 2013/14.

Figure 1
Year-over-year change in world sugar supply and use components: 2014/15 compared with 2013/14

1,000 metric tons, raw value

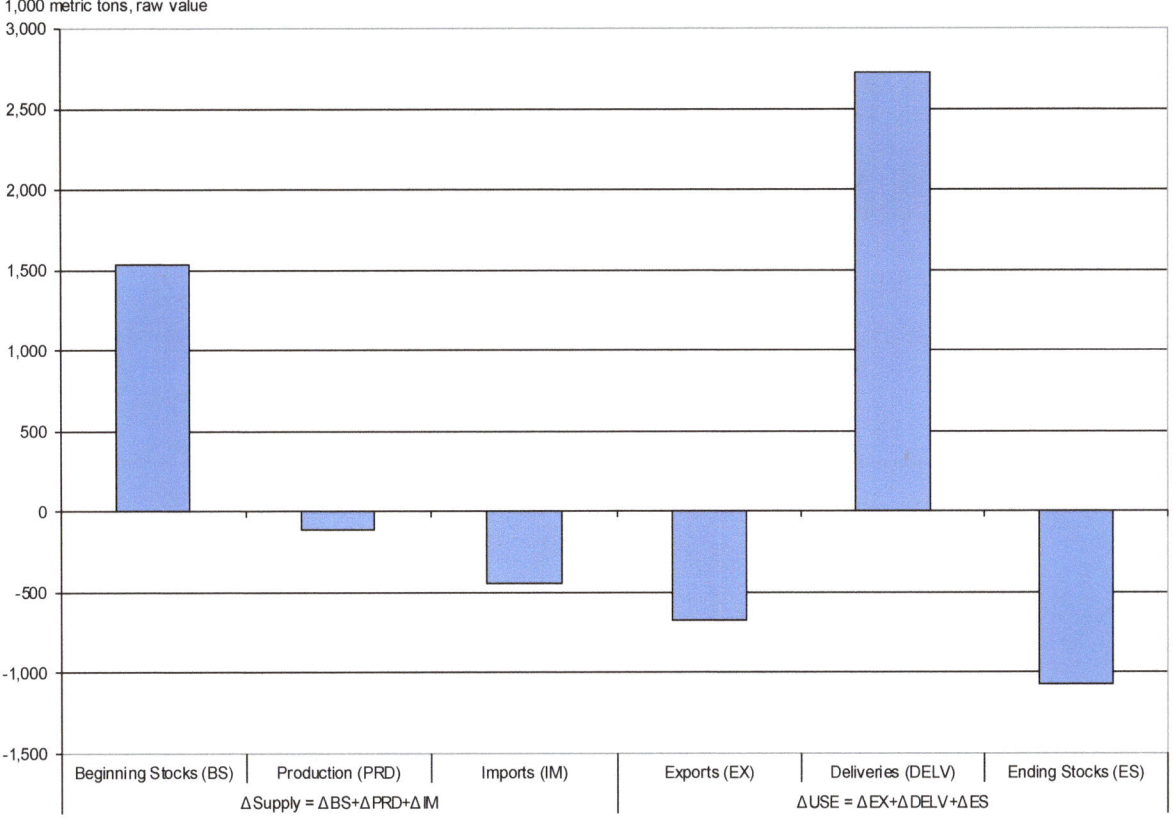

Source: USDA, FAS, PSD database.

Figure 2
World sugar production, consumption, and ending stocks, 2000/01-2014/15

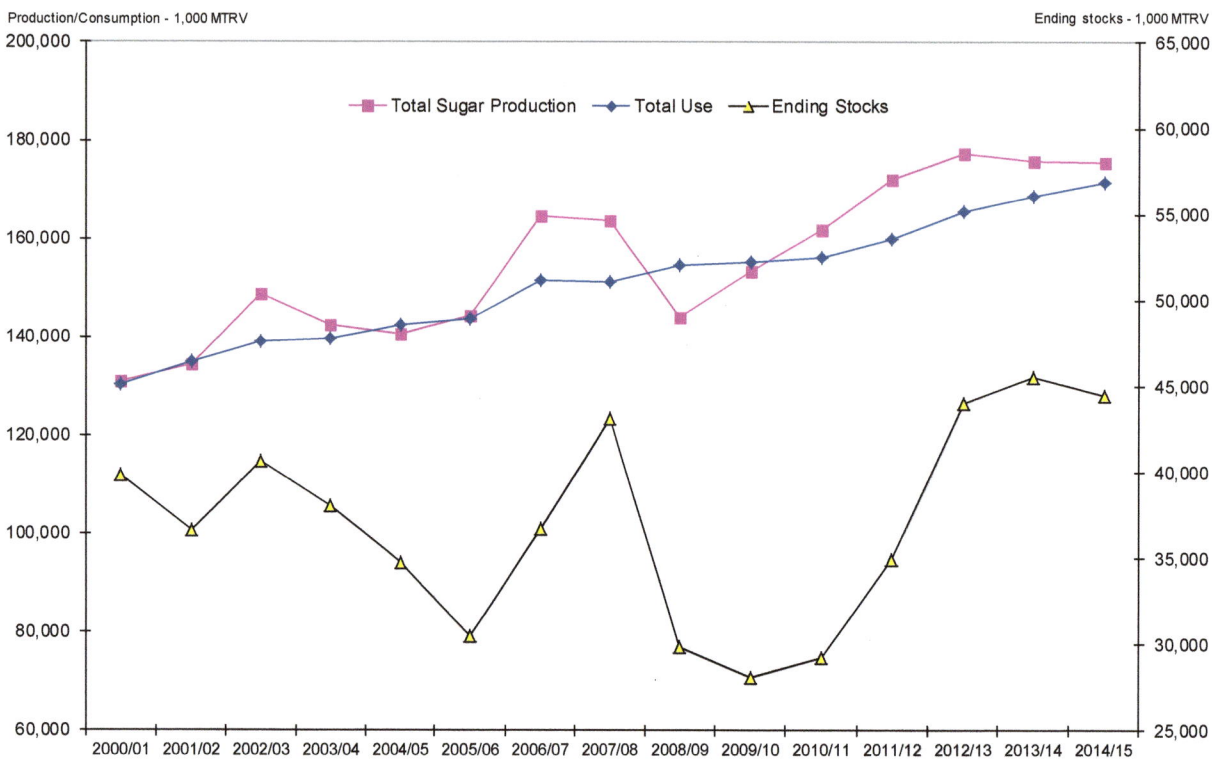

Source: USDA, FAS, PSD database.

Figure 3
World sugar surplus/deficit and stocks-to-use ratios - excess production and growth in world stocks

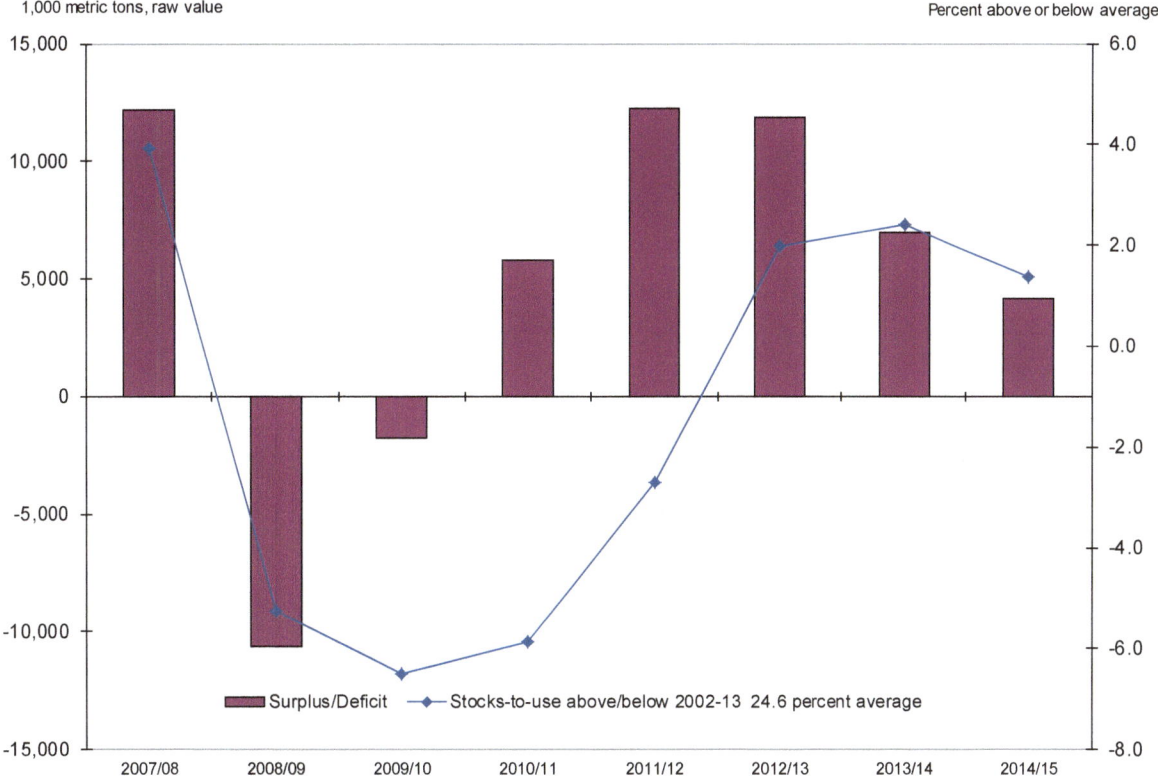

Source: USDA, FAS, PSD database.

The 2014/15 aggregate supply and use balance resembles that of the previous year but with some movement toward less production and fewer ending stocks. Based on these data alone, it would seem difficult to predict radically different world prices in 2014/15.

The May 2014 PSD data represent the latest official estimates and projections made by the USDA. Table 1 shows a comparison of these aggregate supply and use balances with earlier PSD data for 2012/13 and 2013/14. Most data values are close. World production for 2013/14 is estimated somewhat higher than the November 2013 forecast, pushing the 2013/14 world production surplus to 6.969 million MTRV, up from 6.350 million MTRV in November.

Brazil and the World Sugar Export Market

Figure 4 shows the world exports and implied market shares for sugar since 2008/09 for Brazil, other major sugar exporters (Australia, Colombia, Guatemala, South Africa, and Thailand), and all others. Brazil's share has been fairly constant in the 45- to 50-percent range over this period. Brazil's share for projected 2014/15, at 45.7 percent, is at the lower end of the range but not much lower than the country's estimated 46.9 percent share for 2013/14. Other major exporters' share is projected at 27.4 percent, up marginally from 25.0 percent in 2013/14.

Although the Brazilian *real* has deteriorated in value with respect to the U.S. dollar over the course of the last year, its value with respect to other currencies has been more mixed.

Table 1 -- USDA forecast of world sugar supply and use, comparison of current and past forecasts

	2012/13			2013/14			2013/14
	May 2013	November 2013	May 2014	May 2013	November 2013	May 2014	May 2014
				(1,000 metric tons, raw value)			
Beginning Stocks	35,306	35,987	34,949	38,406	43,162	43,978	45,515
Total Sugar Production	174,468	176,033	177,486	174,853	174,826	175,703	175,589
Total Imports	49,926	52,328	51,697	52,305	52,545	50,481	50,037
Total Supply	259,700	264,348	264,132	265,564	270,533	270,162	271,141
Total Exports	56,936	56,561	54,490	59,191	58,678	55,913	55,241
Total Use	164,358	164,625	165,664	168,146	168,476	168,734	171,459
Ending Stocks	38,406	43,162	43,978	38,227	43,379	45,515	44,441
World production surplus (Total production - total use)	10,110	11,408	11,822	6,707	6,350	6,969	4,130
Ending stocks-to-use ratio (percent)	23.4	26.2	26.5	22.7	25.7	27.0	25.9

Source: USDA, FAS, sugar PSD database.

Figure 4
World sugar exports, 2009/10-2014/15

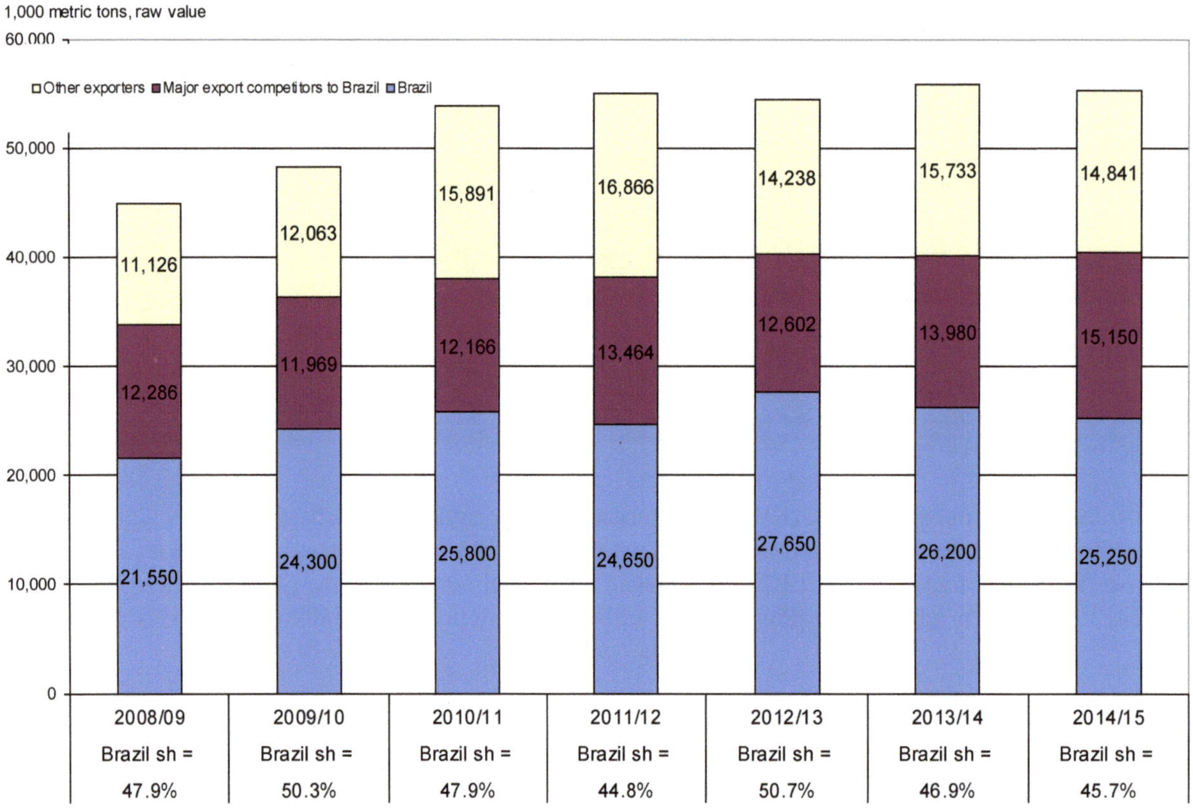

1,000 metric tons, raw value

Source: USDA, FAS, sugar PSD

Major competitors: Australia, Colombia, Guatemala, South Africa, Thailand

The strengthening of currencies in Guatemala and Thailand against the *real* has made their sugar less competitive, while a relative weakening of currencies in South Africa, Indonesia, and even Australia has had the opposite effect for those countries.

The dollar cost of producing sugar in Brazil has a strong influence on world sugar-pricing levels due to Brazil's large share of the world sugar export market. (See Situation and Outlook Report No. SSSM-297-01, May 2013, "World Sugar Prices: The Influence of Brazilian Costs of Production and World Surplus/Deficit Measures.") Figure 5 shows that these costs since 2010/11 have been much higher than earlier years but that costs for 2013/14

Figure 5
Brazil Center/South (C/S) sugar production costs

Index: 2010/11-2012/13 = 100

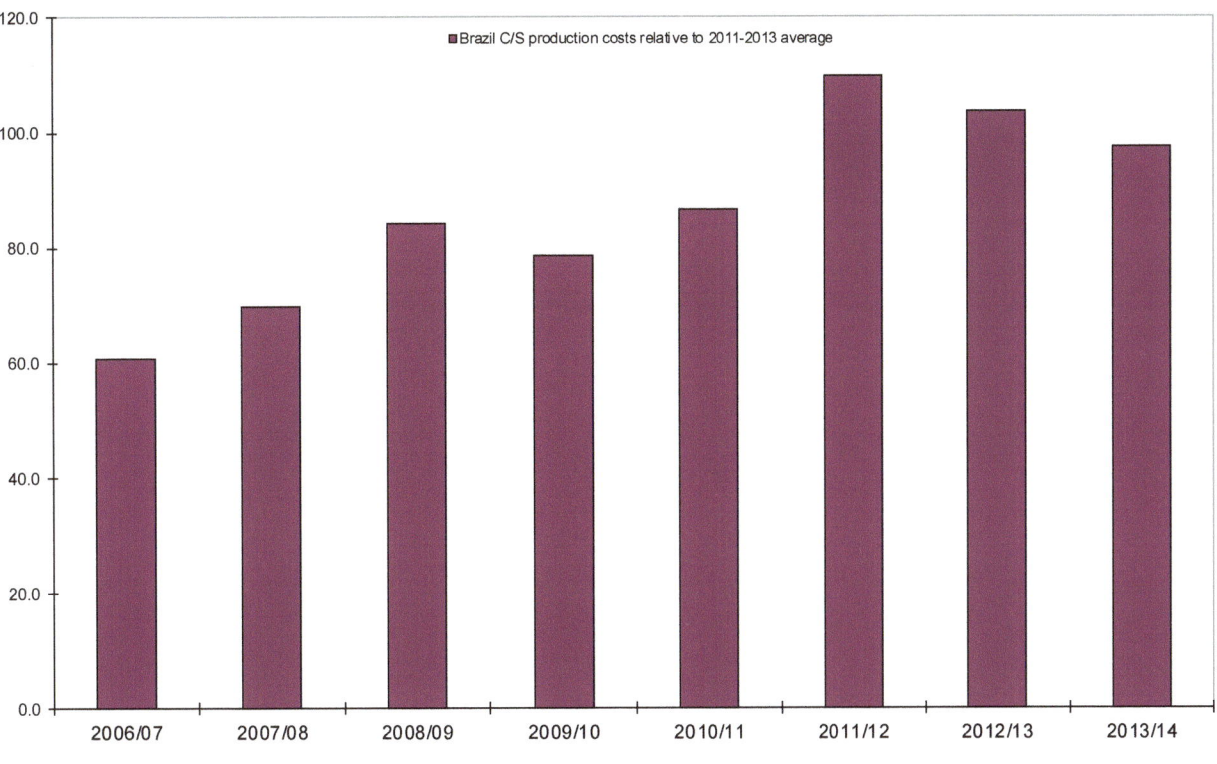

Source: LMC International.

were down relative to the 2 preceding years.[2] Although dependent on exchange rate movements, costs in 2014/15 are not likely to be much different than in the last few years.

Figure 6 shows LMC International estimates of production costs plus FOB (free-on-board) costs for Brazil and other exporting countries. Although Center/South production costs are lower than those of its major competitors, this advantage is undercut by much higher marketing costs in getting the product to export ports for ship loading. The graphic shows only a weak advantage for Brazil and further suggests that combined costs in Thailand are lower than in Brazil.

Many non-USDA analysts and industry participants maintain that Brazil's sugarcane producers are disadvantaged by rising inflation and increasing costs at the start of the 2014/15 season. These observers note that Brazil is plagued by production overcapacity, a lack of storage, and costly transport logistics. Due to high debt levels, many firms rush to sell in the market to generate cash flows to service their immediate by production overcapacity, lack of storage,

---

[2] As noted in earlier editions of the *Sugar and Sweetener* Outlook, LMC International analysis indicates that over the last several years, sugarcane in Center/South Brazil has been aging due to underinvestment in the field. An older crop is more subject to yield variability resulting from less than optimal weather. Also important has been a major switch from manual to mechanical harvesting, which has limited yield growth. Nonetheless, Brazil, especially in the Center/South region, retains cost advantages from large average mill size (economies of scale) and long crushing seasons (high rate of capacity utilization).

Figure 6
Competitiveness in 2013/14 world sugar exports: combined production and fobbing costs relative to Center/South (C/S) Brazil

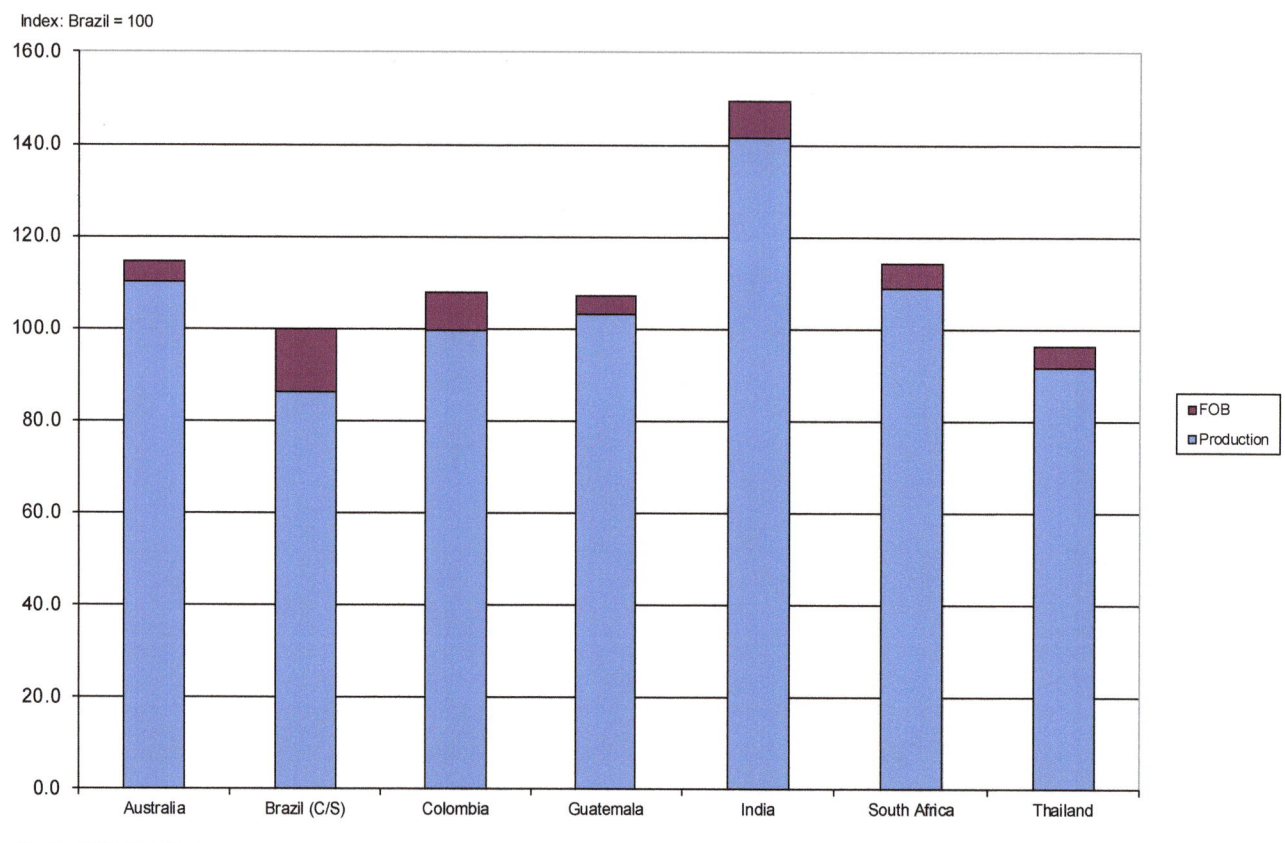

Index: Brazil = 100

Source: LMC International.

debt obligations and lag in developing storage capacity to time their sales for optimal returns. As noted earlier, low Government-determined gasoline prices favor increased sugar production over ethanol that gets sold immediately into the export market, putting downward pressure on world sugar prices. Prospects for policy change that would increase returns for ethanol do not seem good, according to these sources.

U.S. Sweetener Demand

Each year the *Sugar and Sweetener Outlook* of the Economic Research Service (ERS) makes calendar-year estimates of total sweetener deliveries that are available for food and beverage consumption by U.S. consumers. These sweeteners include refined sugar; the corn sweeteners of high fructose corn syrup (HFCS), glucose syrup and dextrose; honey; and other edible syrups, including maple syrup and maple sugar. Table 2 shows new estimates for 2013, along with some revisions for prior years.

U.S. deliveries of total sweeteners for human food and beverage use for 2013 are estimated at 20.314 million tons, almost exactly the same level as in 2012. The increase in refined sugar deliveries of 281,000 tons was offset by corn sweetener decreases of 302,000 tons. Most of the decrease in corn sweeteners was due to a HFCS decrease of 268,000 tons. This decrease continues the downward trend in HFCS consumption and is above the average decrease level since 2003 of 189,000 tons. Both honey and other edible syrups increased about 8,000 tons, on a sucrose-equivalent basis. Moreover, total caloric sweetener deliveries have been in roughly the same 20.0–20.6 million ton range since 2007, with no growth or decline.

On a per capita basis, U.S. sweetener deliveries for 2013 were 128.3 pounds, down 1.0 pounds from 2012 and 20.6 pounds from the 149.0 pounds in 2000. Per capita refined sugar deliveries for human consumption in 2013 were 67.9 pounds, up 1.3 pounds from last year and at their highest level since 1983. The downward trend in corn sweetener use continued with a 2013 decrease of 2.4 pounds. Per capita corn sweetener use has not been at such low levels since 1984.

Sugar contained in net imported products is usually excluded in estimating U.S. per capita sweetener deliveries. Before 1995, sugar contained in imports was offset by sugar in U.S. food exports, indicating only a minor positive adjustment to total deliveries. Beginning in 1995-96, U.S. imports of sugar-containing products started increasing at a faster rate than corresponding product exports. Growth in sugar-containing product imports continued until 2006 but has since leveled off. In 2008, U.S. sugar-containing product exports began to expand, and the estimated amount of per capita sugar in net imports in 2013 stands at only 2.9 pounds, much reduced from the 5.4 pounds in 2006.

Table 3 provides more detail about sugar in imported and exported products. Sugar in imported products in 2013 is estimated at 1.296 million tons, a modest 35,727-ton increase, or 2.8 percent, over 2012. Sugar imported in cocoa and cocoa preparations showed the largest year-over-year increase at 10,255 tons (3.3 percent increase), followed by sugar in sugar confectionery at 9,150 tons (2.3 percent increase) and sugar in bread, pastry, and cakes at 8,619 tons (4.6 percent increase). Sugar in exported products, adjusted for sugar imported under USDA re-export import programs, is estimated at 844,362 tons in 2013, up 62,956 tons from 2012 and 54.5 percent higher than the average level in 2005-07.

Data in the next-to-last column of table 2, estimated by SRI Consulting (now part of the consulting group IHS) and published in their *Chemical Economics Handbook* (CEH), show the sucrose-equivalent availability through 2012 for human consumption of high-intensity sweeteners (HIS) saccharin, aspartame, acesulfame K, sucralose, stevia products, and cyclamate. Unfortunately, this work has not been updated. For that reason, the *Sugar and Sweetener Outlook* made no estimate for 2013.

Table 2 -U.S. total and per capita estimated deliveries of caloric sweeteners for domestic food and beverage use, by calendar year 1/

Calendar year	U.S. population 2/ (July 1) Millions	Refined sugar 3/	HFCS	Corn sweeteners Glucose syrup	Dextrose	Total	Pure honey	Edible syrups	Total caloric sweeteners	Sugar in imported product (SCP)	Total caloric sweeteners incl.SCP	High Intensity Sweeteners 4/ (sucrose equivalence)	Total sweeteners, including high intensity swt.
						1,000 short tons, dry basis							
2000	282.2	9,252	8,822	2,230	476	11,528	157	84	21,021	304	21,325	NA	NA
2001	285.1	9,195	8,870	2,205	469	11,545	134	101	20,975	388	21,363	NA	NA
2002	287.8	9,105	8,998	2,224	473	11,694	153	97	21,049	529	21,579	3,057	24,613
2003	290.3	8,848	8,793	2,209	449	11,451	146	104	20,549	621	21,169	3,191	24,364
2004	293.0	9,029	8,737	2,292	487	11,516	130	96	20,771	656	21,427	3,324	24,814
2005	295.8	9,324	8,709	2,261	481	11,451	156	94	21,024	669	21,694	3,457	25,188
2006	298.8	9,286	8,643	2,053	463	11,159	174	98	20,718	812	21,530	3,591	25,137
2007	301.7	9,230	8,432	2,067	448	10,947	141	94	20,412	777	21,189	3,634	24,757
2008	304.5	9,911	8,021	2,036	419	10,476	151	93	20,631	603	21,234	3,677	24,894
2009	307.2	9,740	7,630	1,991	417	10,038	141	90	20,009	521	20,530	3,933	24,508
2010	309.8	10,208	7,487	1,956	450	9,893	160	104	20,365	643	21,008	4,022	24,948
2011	312.0	10,276	7,282	1,908	446	9,635	169	102	20,183	625	20,808	4,112	24,975
2012	314.3	10,466	7,189	1,969	420	9,579	169	104	20,317	531	20,848	4,201	25,172
2013	316.5	10,747	6,921	1,941	415	9,277	177	112	20,314	452	20,766	NA	NA
						Pounds, dry basis							
2000	282.2	65.6	62.5	15.8	3.4	81.7	1.1	0.6	149.0	2.2	151.1	NA	NA
2001	285.1	64.5	62.2	15.5	3.3	81.0	0.9	0.7	147.1	2.7	149.9	NA	NA
2002	287.8	63.3	62.5	15.5	3.3	81.3	1.1	0.7	146.3	3.7	150.0	21.2	171.0
2003	290.3	61.0	60.6	15.2	3.1	78.9	1.0	0.7	141.6	4.3	145.8	22.0	167.8
2004	293.0	61.6	59.6	15.6	3.3	78.6	0.9	0.7	141.8	4.5	146.2	22.7	169.4
2005	295.8	63.1	58.9	15.3	3.3	77.4	1.1	0.6	142.2	4.5	146.7	23.4	170.3
2006	298.8	62.2	57.8	13.7	3.1	74.7	1.2	0.7	138.7	5.4	144.1	24.0	168.2
2007	301.7	61.2	55.9	13.7	3.0	72.6	0.9	0.6	135.3	5.2	140.5	24.1	164.1
2008	304.5	65.1	52.7	13.4	2.8	68.8	1.0	0.6	135.5	4.0	139.4	24.1	163.5
2009	307.2	63.4	49.7	13.0	2.7	65.3	0.9	0.6	130.3	3.4	133.6	25.6	159.5
2010	309.8	65.9	48.3	12.6	2.9	63.9	1.0	0.7	131.5	4.2	135.6	26.0	161.1
2011	312.0	65.9	46.7	12.2	2.9	61.8	1.1	0.7	129.4	4.0	133.4	26.4	160.1
2012	314.3	66.6	45.7	12.5	2.7	61.0	1.1	0.7	129.3	3.4	132.7	26.7	160.2
2013	316.5	67.9	43.7	12.3	2.6	58.6	1.1	0.7	128.3	2.9	131.2	NA	NA

1/ Per capita deliveries of sweeteners by U.S. processors and refiners and direct-consumption imports to food manufacturers, retailers, and other end users represent the per capita supply of caloric sweeteners. The data exclude deliveries to manufacturers of alcoholic beverages. Actual human intake of caloric sweeteners is lower because of uneaten food, spoilage, and other losses. See Table 51 of the Sugar and Sweeteners Yearbook series for estimated intake of sugar.
2/ Source: U.S. Census Bureau
3/ Based on U.S. sugar deliveries for domestic food and beverage use.
4/ SRI Consulting, Chemical Economics Handbook, High-Intensity Sweeteners Market Research Report, May 2010.
Source: USDA, ERS, Sugar and Sweeteners Outlook.

Per Capita Consumption/Intake

The Food Availability Data System developed by USDA's Economic Research Service (ERS) tracks annual food and nutrient availability in the United States, beginning with 1909 data, for several hundred commodities, including sugar and other added sweeteners (as discussed above). Because the core Food Availability data series in the system overstates actual consumption, ERS added another series to the system—the Loss-Adjusted Food Availability data—that adjusts the data to account for nonedible food parts and food losses, including losses from farm to retail, at retail, and at the consumer level. This second data series more closely estimates per capita food intake.

Table 4 shows the derivation of intake consumption for refined sugar, high fructose corn syrup, and the other added sugars. The primary weight (first data column) is taken from the sweetener availabilities seen in the bottom panel of table 2. Although there are four loss categories, only two of these are relevant for added sugars: loss from retail to consumer level and loss at the consumer level for uneaten portions, spoilage, etc. The retail-to-consumer loss is estimated at 11 percent for all sweeteners. Consumer-level losses are 34 percent for refined sugar and corn sweeteners and 15 percent for honey and edible syrups. The next columns translate the annual consumption (pounds) into daily levels, i.e., ounces and grams per day. The last two columns show the implied daily calorie consumption and the corresponding number of equivalent teaspoons of sugar consumed daily.

Per capita refined sugar consumption for 2013 is estimated at 41.6 pounds, up 0.5 pounds from last year. (This amount includes sugar consumed in imported products.) Per capita HFCS consumption has been decreasing steadily since 2000 and its value in 2013 is estimated at 25.7 pounds, down 1.2 pounds from 2012 and 11.0 pounds since 2000.

Table 3 -- Estimated sugar in U.S. product imports and exports, 1995-2013.

Year	Sugar Confectionery	Cocoa and Cocoa Preparations	Cereal and Bakers Preparations	Bread, Pastry, Cakes, etc.	Misc. Edible Preparations	Carbonated Soft Drinks	Total sugar in imported products	Total sugar in exported products	Sugar in exported products less USDA product re-export program sugar	Domestic consumption of sugar in imported products
					1,000 short tons					
1995	137,760	66,265	6,286	43,705	68,945	26,405	349,365	317,809	228,286	121,079
1996	148,383	75,911	8,580	49,882	60,729	32,456	375,940	356,966	259,704	116,236
1997	161,894	92,664	14,273	64,812	68,172	39,403	441,218	390,159	244,221	196,997
1998	186,572	97,616	19,110	74,726	91,119	39,811	508,954	371,414	234,786	274,168
1999	223,421	111,807	20,116	87,875	118,876	48,165	610,261	392,208	256,467	353,794
2000	239,914	130,407	19,548	99,740	120,366	58,745	668,719	442,596	364,435	304,284
2001	259,975	160,350	18,097	115,917	127,331	64,961	746,630	470,991	358,723	387,907
2002	299,003	193,608	19,419	117,838	140,369	70,852	841,090	459,931	311,921	529,169
2003	362,786	208,260	25,139	134,500	150,859	83,440	964,985	507,950	344,232	620,753
2004	400,819	220,067	25,082	138,898	186,328	97,731	1,068,925	539,237	413,071	655,854
2005	456,969	231,322	26,012	143,742	187,838	109,747	1,155,630	596,960	486,288	669,342
2006	499,547	275,449	24,732	148,595	193,692	126,714	1,268,728	560,835	456,902	811,826
2007	433,062	276,990	25,081	150,538	189,345	128,811	1,260,363	588,293	426,578	833,785
2008	408,183	271,271	23,698	154,799	186,760	123,355	1,168,066	680,094	564,567	603,499
2009	381,207	256,855	16,335	157,347	169,954	112,489	1,094,186	696,963	573,504	520,682
2010	404,539	289,914	16,878	174,031	182,468	125,217	1,193,046	741,699	550,078	642,969
2011	400,910	315,141	16,661	184,366	188,218	135,070	1,240,367	820,802	615,630	624,737
2012	402,879	309,577	16,851	188,643	183,624	159,331	1,260,905	836,213	729,756	531,149
2013	412,030	319,832	18,979	197,262	182,298	166,230	1,296,632	899,169	844,362	452,270

Source: USDA, ERS, Sugar and Sweetener Outlook.

Table 4 -- Added sugar: estimated number of per capita calories consumed daily, by calendar year 1/

Sweetener/ Year	Primary weight (market level) 2/	Loss from primary to retail weight	Weight at retail level	Loss from retail/institutional to consumer level	Weight at consumer level	Loss at consumer level Nonedible share	Other (uneaten food, spoilage, etc.)	Per capita consumption, adjusted for loss			Calories per serving (teaspoon)	Serving weight	Calories consumed daily 3/	Servings (teaspoons) consumed daily 4/
	lb/yr	percent	lb/yr	percent	lb/yr	percent	percent	lb/yr	oz/day	g/day	number	grams	number	teaspoons
Refined sugar														
2000	67.7	0.0	67.7	11.0	60.3	0.0	34.0	39.8	1.7	49.4	16.0	4.2	188	11.8
2001	67.2	0.0	67.2	11.0	59.8	0.0	34.0	39.5	1.7	49.1	16.0	4.2	187	11.7
2002	66.9	0.0	66.9	11.0	59.6	0.0	34.0	39.3	1.7	48.9	16.0	4.2	186	11.6
2003	65.2	0.0	65.2	11.0	58.1	0.0	34.0	38.3	1.7	47.6	16.0	4.2	181	11.3
2004	66.1	0.0	66.1	11.0	58.8	0.0	34.0	38.8	1.7	48.2	16.0	4.2	184	11.5
2005	67.6	0.0	67.6	11.0	60.1	0.0	34.0	39.7	1.7	49.3	16.0	4.2	188	11.7
2006	67.6	0.0	67.6	11.0	60.2	0.0	34.0	39.7	1.7	49.3	16.0	4.2	188	11.7
2007	66.3	0.0	66.3	11.0	59.0	0.0	34.0	39.0	1.7	48.4	16.0	4.2	184	11.5
2008	69.1	0.0	69.1	11.0	61.5	0.0	34.0	40.6	1.8	50.4	16.0	4.2	192	12.0
2009	66.8	0.0	66.8	11.0	59.4	0.0	34.0	39.2	1.7	48.8	16.0	4.2	186	11.6
2010	70.1	0.0	70.1	11.0	62.4	0.0	34.0	41.2	1.8	51.1	16.0	4.2	195	12.2
2011	69.9	0.0	69.9	11.0	62.2	0.0	34.0	41.0	1.8	51.0	16.0	4.2	194	12.1
2012	70.0	0.0	70.0	11.0	62.3	0.0	34.0	41.1	1.8	51.1	16.0	4.2	195	12.2
2013	70.8	0.0	70.8	11.0	63.0	0.0	34.0	41.6	1.8	51.7	16.0	4.2	197	12.3
High Fructose Corn Syrup (HFCS)														
2000	62.5	0.0	62.5	11.0	55.6	0.0	34.0	36.7	1.6	45.6	16.0	4.2	174	10.9
2001	62.2	0.0	62.2	11.0	55.4	0.0	34.0	36.6	1.6	45.4	16.0	4.2	173	10.8
2002	62.5	0.0	62.5	11.0	55.6	0.0	34.0	36.7	1.6	45.6	16.0	4.2	174	10.9
2003	60.6	0.0	60.6	11.0	53.9	0.0	34.0	35.6	1.6	44.2	16.0	4.2	168	10.5
2004	59.6	0.0	59.6	11.0	53.1	0.0	34.0	35.0	1.5	43.5	16.0	4.2	166	10.4
2005	58.9	0.0	58.9	11.0	52.4	0.0	34.0	34.6	1.5	43.0	16.0	4.2	164	10.2
2006	57.8	0.0	57.8	11.0	51.5	0.0	34.0	34.0	1.5	42.2	16.0	4.2	161	10.1
2007	55.9	0.0	55.9	11.0	49.7	0.0	34.0	32.8	1.4	40.8	16.0	4.2	155	9.7
2008	52.7	0.0	52.7	11.0	46.9	0.0	34.0	30.9	1.4	38.5	16.0	4.2	146	9.2
2009	49.7	0.0	49.7	11.0	44.2	0.0	34.0	29.2	1.3	36.3	16.0	4.2	138	8.6
2010	48.3	0.0	48.3	11.0	43.0	0.0	34.0	28.4	1.2	35.3	16.0	4.2	134	8.4
2011	46.7	0.0	46.7	11.0	41.5	0.0	34.0	27.4	1.2	34.1	16.0	4.2	130	8.1
2012	45.7	0.0	45.7	11.0	40.7	0.0	34.0	26.9	1.2	33.4	16.0	4.2	127	8.0
2013	43.7	0.0	43.7	11.0	38.9	0.0	34.0	25.7	1.1	31.9	16.0	4.2	122	7.6
Other added sweeteners, including glucose syrup, dextrose, honey, and edible syrups														
2000	20.9	0.0	20.9	11.0	18.6	0.0	32.4	12.6	0.6	15.6	16.0	4.2	59	3.7
2001	20.4	0.0	20.4	11.0	18.2	0.0	32.5	12.3	0.5	15.2	16.0	4.2	58	3.6
2002	20.5	0.0	20.5	11.0	18.2	0.0	32.4	12.3	0.5	15.3	16.0	4.2	58	3.6
2003	20.0	0.0	20.0	11.0	17.8	0.0	32.4	12.1	0.5	15.0	16.0	4.2	57	3.6
2004	20.5	0.0	20.5	11.0	18.3	0.0	32.6	12.3	0.5	15.3	16.0	4.2	58	3.6
2005	20.2	0.0	20.2	11.0	18.0	0.0	32.4	12.2	0.5	15.1	16.0	4.2	58	3.6
2006	18.7	0.0	18.7	11.0	16.6	0.0	32.1	11.3	0.5	14.0	16.0	4.2	53	3.3
2007	18.2	0.0	18.2	11.0	16.2	0.0	32.4	11.0	0.5	13.6	16.0	4.2	52	3.2
2008	17.7	0.0	17.7	11.0	15.8	0.0	32.3	10.7	0.5	13.3	16.0	4.2	51	3.2
2009	17.2	0.0	17.2	11.0	15.3	0.0	32.3	10.3	0.5	12.9	16.0	4.2	49	3.1
2010	17.2	0.0	17.2	11.0	15.3	0.0	32.1	10.4	0.5	12.9	16.0	4.2	49	3.1
2011	16.8	0.0	16.8	11.0	15.0	0.0	32.0	10.2	0.4	12.6	16.0	4.2	48	3.0
2012	16.9	0.0	16.9	11.0	15.1	0.0	34.0	10.0	0.4	12.4	16.0	4.2	47	2.9
2013	16.7	0.0	16.7	11.0	14.9	0.0	34.0	9.8	0.4	12.2	16.0	4.2	46	2.9
Total added sweeteners														
2000	151.1	0.0	151.1	11.0	134.5	0.0	33.8	89.1	3.9	110.7	16.0	4.2	422	26.4
2001	149.9	0.0	149.9	11.0	133.4	0.0	33.8	88.3	3.9	109.7	16.0	4.2	418	26.1
2002	150.0	0.0	150.0	11.0	133.5	0.0	33.8	88.4	3.9	109.8	16.0	4.2	418	26.1
2003	145.8	0.0	145.8	11.0	129.8	0.0	33.8	86.0	3.8	106.8	16.0	4.2	407	25.4
2004	146.2	0.0	146.2	11.0	130.2	0.0	33.8	86.2	3.8	107.1	16.0	4.2	408	25.5
2005	146.7	0.0	146.7	11.0	130.6	0.0	33.8	86.5	3.8	107.4	16.0	4.2	409	25.6
2006	144.1	0.0	144.1	11.0	128.2	0.0	33.8	85.0	3.7	105.6	16.0	4.2	402	25.1
2007	140.5	0.0	140.5	11.0	125.0	0.0	33.8	82.8	3.6	102.9	16.0	4.2	392	24.5
2008	139.4	0.0	139.4	11.0	124.1	0.0	33.8	82.2	3.6	102.1	16.0	4.2	389	24.3
2009	133.6	0.0	133.6	11.0	118.9	0.0	33.8	78.8	3.5	97.9	16.0	4.2	373	23.3
2010	135.6	0.0	135.6	11.0	120.7	0.0	33.8	80.0	3.5	99.4	16.0	4.2	379	23.7
2011	133.4	0.0	133.4	11.0	118.7	0.0	33.8	78.6	3.4	97.7	16.0	4.2	372	23.3
2012	132.7	0.0	132.7	11.0	118.1	0.0	34.0	77.9	3.4	96.8	16.0	4.2	369	23.1
2013	131.2	0.0	131.2	11.0	116.8	0.0	34.0	77.1	3.4	95.8	16.0	4.2	365	22.8

1/ Estimated number of daily per capita calories calculated by adjusting sweetener deliveries for domestic food and beverage use for food losses, includes sugar in imported products.
2/ U.S. per capita cane and beet sugar estimated deliveries for domestic food and beverage use, calendar year. See Table 50 of Sugar and Sweetener Yearbook series.
3/ Number of daily teaspoons multiplied by calories per serving.
4/ Grams per day divided by serving weight.

Source: USDA, ERS, Sugar and Sweeteners Outlook.

Consumption of other added sugars has decreased, as well. Overall, per capita sweetener intake for 2013 is at 77.1 pounds, down 0.8 pounds from 2012 and 12.0 pounds from 2000. In terms of daily calories, the 2013 intake is 365 calories—a reduction in sweetener intake of about 13.5 percent compared with the 422 calories estimated for 2000.

Sugar and Sweeteners Outlook/SSS-M-310/June 18, 2014
Economic Research Service, USDA

Effect of Direct Consumption Sugar Imports from Mexico on Domestic Sweetener Deliveries

The primary cause of reduced HFCS deliveries since 1999 has been a decrease in the consumption of carbonated soft drinks as consumers switched to alternatives such as bottled water. The largest effect was on HFCS55, the main sweetener ingredient in soft drinks. Much less affected was HFCS42 because a much smaller proportion of it is used as a sweetening agent in soft drinks. Between 1999 and 2007, the average per capita HFCS42 consumption held steady between 23-24 pounds. In 2008, the same year as the full implementation of the sweetener provisions of the North American Free Trade Agreement (NAFTA), consumption of HFCS42 started a steep decline from 21.32 pounds in 2008 to 16.03 pounds in 2013. At the same time, per capita refined sugar consumption increased from 61.2 pounds in 2007 to 67.9 pounds in 2013.

Until 2012/13, most sugar imports from Mexico were intended for direct consumption and not as raw sugar for refining. The implication is that this sugar from Mexico became competitive with other domestically produced sweeteners for end user demand. One way to examine this issue is to see if there are negative statistical relationships between those direct consumption sugar imports from Mexico and sugar and HFCS deliveries from domestic processors and refiners. Table A-2 in the appendix details the approach and presents results for the three sweeteners where the relationship was found statistically significant; that is, for HFCS42, HFCS55, and beet sugar deliveries to industrial end users.

Figure 7 interprets the results graphically by showing on an annual basis how much of those sweeteners were displaced by the imports. It is clear that HFCS42 was the most negatively affected, followed by HFCS55 and then beet sugar to industrial users. Average annual displacement over the period 2008 through 2013 for HFCS42 was 326,817 tons, dry weight; for HFCS55, 155,103 tons; and beet sugar, 110,615 tons. Over four times the quantity of HFCS was displaced relative to beet sugar. On a percentage basis, HFCS42 deliveries decreased by about 10 percent below what they would have been otherwise. A comparable percentage for HFCS55 is 3.3 percent, and for beet sugar, 2.5 percent.

Figure 7
Estimated market displacement of direct consumption sugar imports from Mexico since the implementation of NAFTA sugar provisions

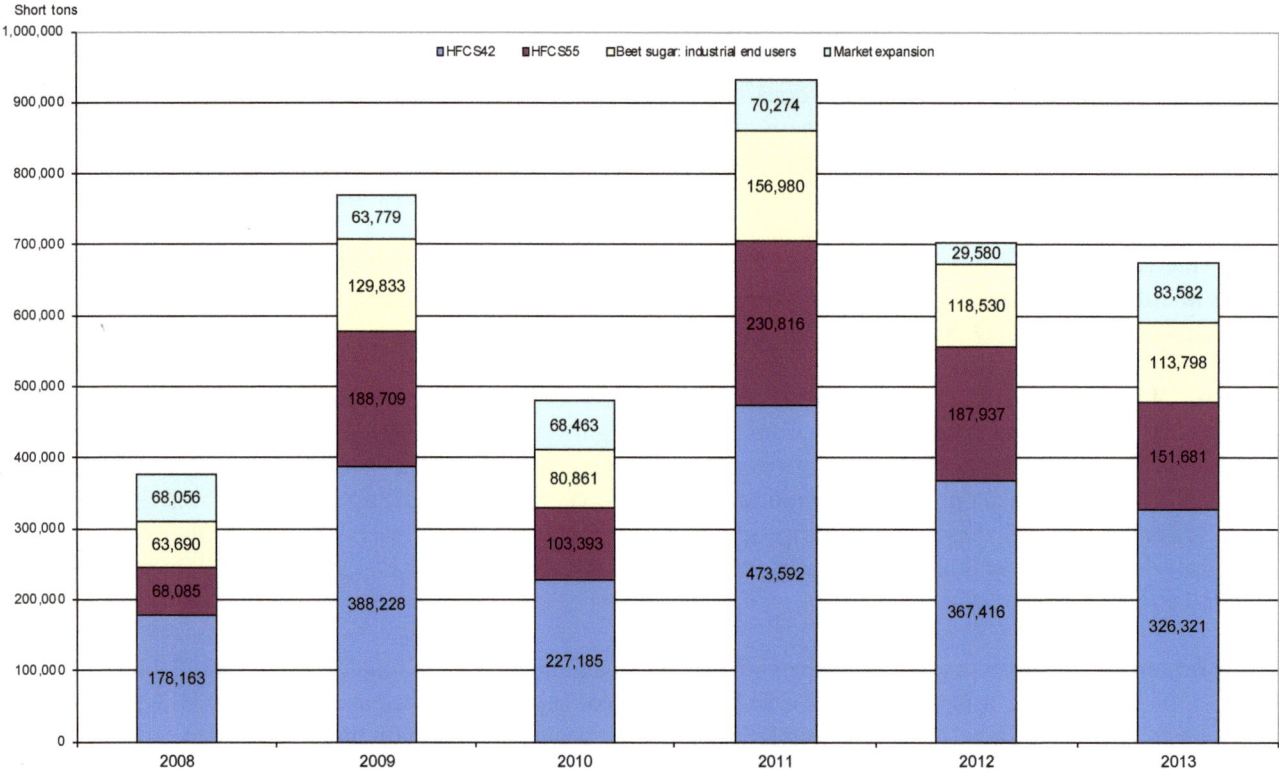

Source: Sugar and Sweetener Outlook.

NAFTA Sugar and High Fructose Corn Syrup Production Costs

Last month the Sugar and Sweetener Outlook of the Economic Research Service (ERS) analyzed sweetener cost of production data for the last decade from LMC International. These data included costs of producing cane sugar, beet sugar, and High Fructose Corn Syrup for almost all producing countries in the world. [1] As mentioned in the report, LMC International presents costs for regions within certain important producing countries. Included in the set are regional costs for cane sugar in the United States and Mexico and for beet sugar in the United States. Costs of producing High Fructose Corn Syrup (HFCS) in both countries are presented as well. This chapter provides a quick overview of these costs for both of these countries, whose sweetener markets are covered under the sweetener provisions of the North American Free Trade Agreement (NAFTA).

Table 5 shows how LMC International classifies the regions, how much sugar (or HFCS) is produced, and the relative shares as a proportion of total sugar and total sweeteners (that is, refined sugar plus HFCS). [2][3] Figure 8 shows the aggregate regional data and shares. In the combined NAFTA market, HFCS production has the largest share and most of this production is located in the United States. The Mexico cane sector is larger than either the U.S. beet sugar or cane sugar sectors but smaller than the combined U.S. sugar sectors. As a percentage of total sweetener production, Mexico's share is only about 30 percent.

For sugar, the largest producing region is Mexico's Gulf (mostly Veracruz), followed by Red River Valley for beet sugar, and for cane sugar, Florida and Louisiana and Mexico's Pacific region (Jalisco, Michoácan, and others), followed by Mexico's Northeast (mainly San Luis Potosi and Tamaulipas).

Table 6 shows ranges of sweetener production costs corresponding to four 3-year intervals, starting at 2001/02 and ending in 2012/13. The cane sugar is classified as Low Cost Mexico (all regions but the Northwest), U.S. Mainland, and High-Cost NAFTA (Hawaii and Mexico's Northwest). The low end of the HFCS production cost range has been the lowest in all four of the period intervals, averaging between 80 and 90 percent of the next highest low-end value (either Low-Cost Mexico or U.S. Mainland). Low-end values in all sweetener classifications have been increasing over time, with the exception of beet sugar costs from 2007/08-2009/10 to 2010/11-2012/13. This has been especially true for cane's High-Cost NAFTA, but its share of the overall sweetener production is fairly small.

Figure 9 shows relative regional costs for the 2010/11-2012/13 period based on averaged values, along with production quantities, from lowest cost (HFCS) to highest (High Cane-Cost NAFTA). Average costs of beet sugar are indexed to equal 100, and all other regional costs are defined with respect to it. HFCS costs are at 83 percent of the beet costs. Although the midpoint range of Low-Cost Mexico at $507/mt is

---

[1] LMC International's *Sugar and HFS Production Costs* is copyrighted, and results for specific countries or regions may not be quoted or published without prior approval of LMC International. For detailed information regarding LMC International services, contact: LMC International, 1841 Broadway, New York, NY, 10023. Tel: 202-586-2427, info@lmc-ny.com.

[2] For technical reasons, LMC International excludes beet sugar from desugared molasses in its production totals. Their cost of production methodology treats the sugar sales revenue from desugared molasses as a byproduct credit when calculating net production costs.

[3] Cane sugar production and production costs are shown in terms of white, or refined, value. The metric ton cost of refining is assumed to be $65 per metric ton.

Table 5 -- U.S. and Mexico sugar producing areas

Sweetener categories	Other designation	States	Average production: 2010/11-2012/13	Percent of total sugar	Percent of total sweetener
			(1,000 metric tons, white value)		
U.S. beet sugar areas					
Central Great Plains	Beet	Colorado, Nebraska, SE Wyoming	258	2.0	1.2
Great Lakes	Beet	Michigan	488	3.9	2.3
Northern Great Plains	Beet	Montana, NE Wyoming, western North Dakota	271	2.2	1.3
Northwest	Beet	Idaho, Oregon, Washington	721	5.7	3.4
Red River Valley	Beet	Minnesota, eastern North Dakota	1,883	15.0	8.9
Southwest	Beet	California	126	1.0	0.6
U.S. cane sugar areas					
Florida	U.S. Mainland		1,449	11.5	6.8
Louisiana	U.S. Mainland		1,282	10.2	6.1
Texas	U.S. Mainland		132	1.1	0.6
Hawaii	High cane cost NAFTA		151	1.2	0.7
Mexico cane sugar areas 1/					
Central	Low cost cane	Morelos (2), Puebla (2)	458	3.6	2.2
Gulf	Low cost cane	Oaxaca (3), Veracruz (20)	2,329	18.5	11.0
Northeast	Low cost cane	San LuisPotosi (4), Tamalispas (2), NE Veracruz (2)	1,090	8.7	5.1
Northwest	High cane cost NAFTA	Sinaloa (3)	137	1.1	0.6
Pacific	Low cost cane	Colima (1), Jalisco (6), Michoacan (4), Nayarit (2)	1,256	10.0	5.9
South	Low cost cane	Campeche (1), Chiapas (2), Oaxaca (1), Tabasco (3), Quintana Roo (1)	561	4.5	2.7
NAFTA HFCS			8,578		40.5

Source: LMC International.
1/ The numbers in parenthese indicate the number of factories in the Mexican States in the regional categories.

Table 6 -- Ranges of average costs of producing cane sugar, beet sugar, and high fructose syrup, by select categories of NAFTA producers, 2001/02-2012/13.

	2001/02-2003/04		2004/05-2006/07		2007/08-2009/10		2010/11-2012/13	
				Dollars/mt				
	Min	Max	Min	Max	Min	Max	Min	Max
Cane sugar (white sugar equiv.)								
Low cost Mexico	295.2	338.9	303.7	438.0	366.9	558.1	383.7	632.2
U.S. mainland	231.4	475.9	305.1	604.4	347.5	692.6	424.3	693.7
High cost NAFTA	346.6	434.0	419.7	622.9	486.8	834.6	660.6	760.2
Beet sugar	383.0	678.3	412.2	689.2	439.4	854.8	412.1	733.7
HFCS	215.6	308.9	245.4	432.9	310.4	593.7	326.8	681.9

Source: LMC International.

much below the corresponding beet sugar midpoint of $573/mt, averaged Low-Cost Mexico is 13 percent higher than the average U.S. beet sugar costs. As seen below, this reflects the high proportion of beet sugar production from the very low-cost Red River Valley. U.S. Mainland cane costs are a bit higher than costs in the Mexico cane category. Costs in High-Cost NAFTA are much higher—55 percent relative to beet sugar—but as mentioned, very little sugar is produced in these regions.

The production-weighted average of sugar production costs in 2010/11-2012/13 is $554/mt. Figure 10 shows the distribution of costs around this average for all sugar-producing regions. Costs are especially low in the Red River Valley and the beet-producing U.S. Northwest, in Mexico's Central region, and in Florida. Mexico's other main cane-producing regions have costs centered around the average. Costs are much higher in Hawaii and Mexico's Northwest, but costs in Louisiana (a large producer), Texas, and Northern Great Plains are not that much lower in comparison.

Figure 8
Average NAFTA sweetener production, 2010/11-2012/13

Average sweetener production = 21.168 million mt, white equiv.

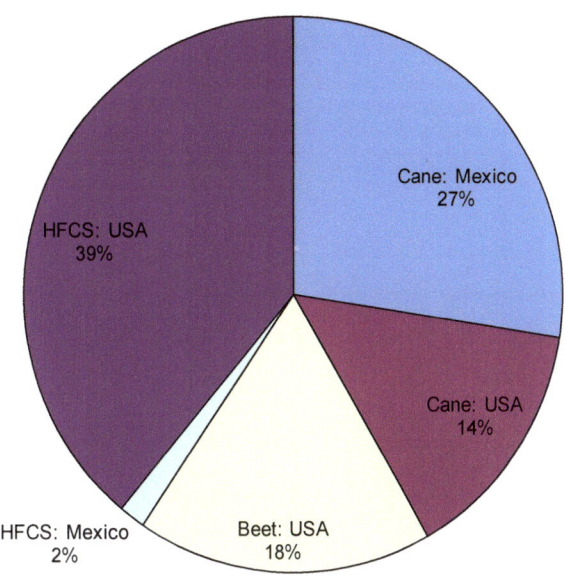

Source: LMC International.

Figure 9
Distribution of NAFTA sweetener production costs by type of producer, 2010/11-2012/13

Beet sugar cost = 100

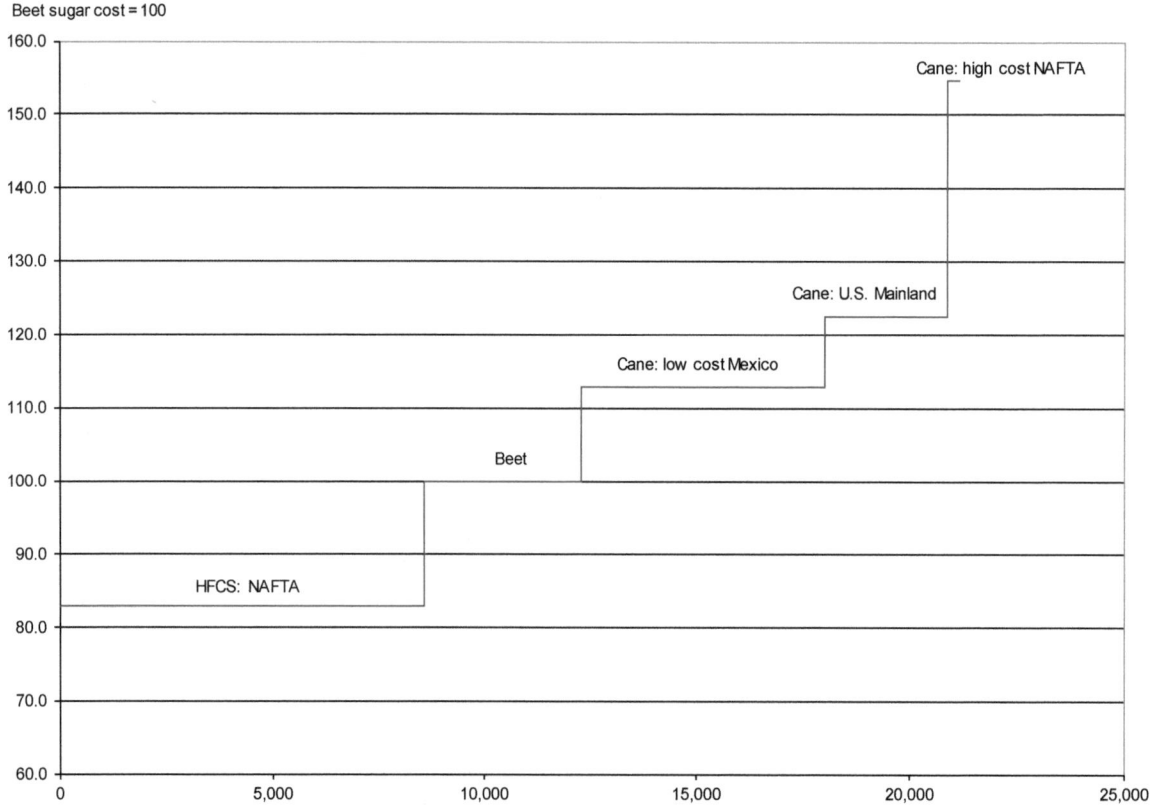

Metric tons, white sugar equivalent

Figure 10
Sugar production costs in the NAFTA: percent above/below average costs, white value (wv), 2010/11-2012/13

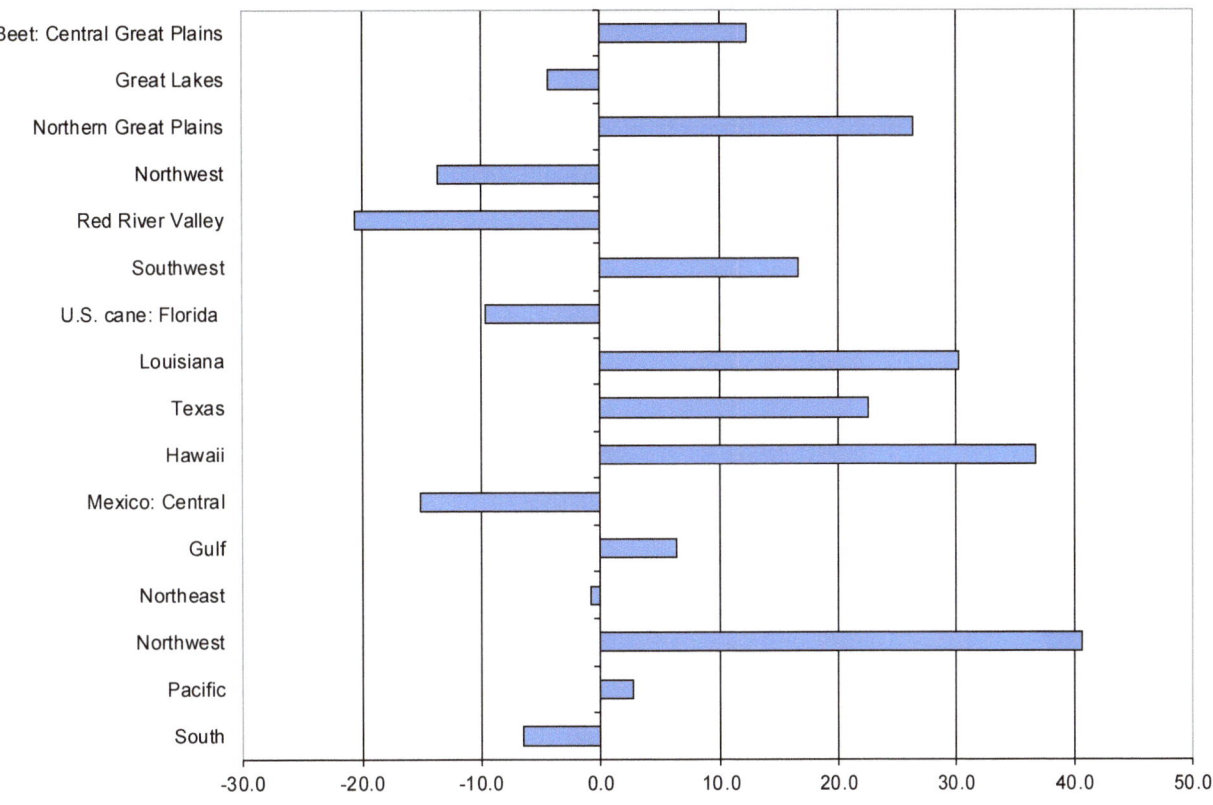

Source: LMC International.

Percent above/below weighted average cost: $554/mt, wv.

Figure 11
Comparison of NAFTA sweetener production components for 2010/11-2012/13, including byproduct credits

Index: Mexico cane = 100.0

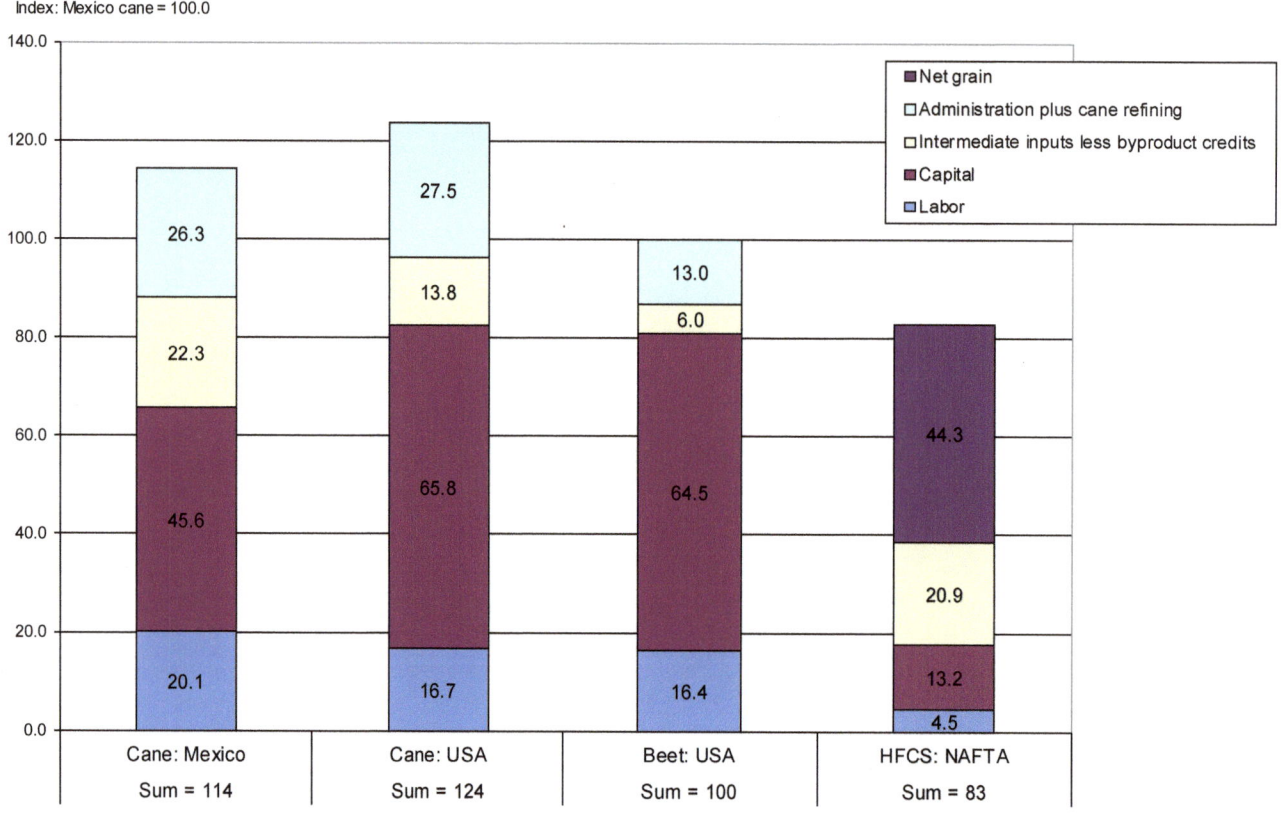

Source: LMC International.

Figure 11, like figure 9, illustrates relative costs among the main producing regions (U.S. and Mexico cane sectors here include the high-cost areas) but focuses on the factor shares' contribution to the total. In the U.S. sectors, capital costs constitute a higher proportion of the total than in Mexico, implying that cash costs are lower in U.S. cane production than in Mexico. Intermediate costs (fuel, fertilizer, other inputs) less byproduct credits (mainly molasses) are higher in Mexico. Labor costs are low in all regions. The largest component of HFCS costs are net corn costs. These costs have contributed the most to HFCS cost increases over the last 10 years and make those costs volatile (although still lower than the sugar costs).

Figure 12 shows aggregated NAFTA sugar and sweetener costs and the respective trends over the 2001/02–2012/13 period. In the first 3 years of the period, sugar costs averaged $400.15/mt, while the average in the final 3 years was $553.79/mt, an increase of 38.4 percent. In the first 3 years of the period, total sweetener costs that include HFCS averaged $324.89/mt, while the average in the final 3 years was $495.20/mt, an increase of 52.4 percent. Inclusion of relatively low HFCS costs lowers the average, but the fact that HFCS costs have been increasing at a higher rate than sugar indicates a higher growth rate. This can also be seen in that the trend growth of sweeteners has been $19.70/mt per year, while the sugar cost-trend growth has been about $2 lower at $17.98/mt per year.

Figure 12
NAFTA average sugar and sweetener costs of production - wt. average of cane and beet, and HFCS

Dollars/mt, white equiv.

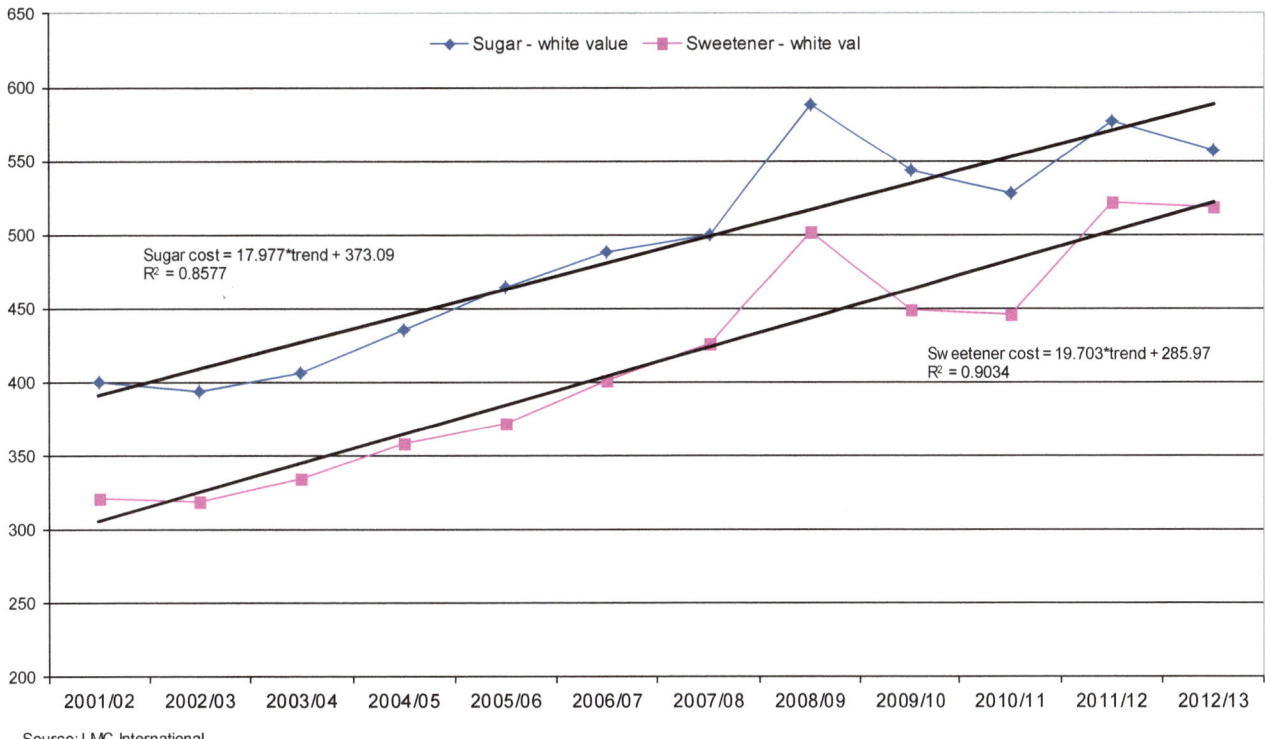

Source: LMC International.

Sugar and Sweeteners in the North American Free Trade Area

On June 11, 2014, the U.S. Department of Agriculture (USDA) published in the *World Agricultural Supply and Demand Estimates* (WASDE) its latest sugar supply and use estimates/projections for Mexico (table 7) and for the United States (table 8) for the October/September fiscal years 2013/14 and 2014/15.

The USDA lowered its estimate of Mexico 2013/14 sugar production from last month by 250,000 metric tons (mt) to 6.100 million mt as output continues to lag well behind the pace forecast by Mexico's *Comite Nacional Para El Desarrollo Sustentable de la Caña de Azucar* (Conadesuca). Given lower supplies, the USDA reduced its estimate of total exports by 121,000 mt to 2.278 million mt. Even so, the USDA expects that exports to the United States will increase from last month by 129,000 mt to 1.708 million mt, based on the pace to date. Exports to the rest of the world are forecast correspondingly lower. As a consequence, ending stocks are expected to fall by 129,000 mt to 818,000 mt, or 19.0 percent of consumption.

For 2014/15, the USDA forecasts Mexico sugar exports to decline by 129,000 mt to match the decrease in beginning stocks. No other supply or use forecast component was changed. However, because of relatively higher prices expected in the U.S. sugar market, the USDA raised its forecast of exports to the United States by 591,000 mt to 1.807 million. Exports to other countries are forecast at only 100,000 mt in 2014/15. The USDA forecasts ending stocks in 2014/15 at 22.0 percent of domestic consumption, or 947,000 mt, the same as last month.

The USDA estimates that total 2013/14 U.S. sugar supply will rise by 261,000 short tons, raw value (STRV), with a 10,000 STRV increase in sugar from production in Texas and a 251,000 STRV increase in imports. Imports under the re-export program were raised 100,000 STRV, based on industry estimates, and imports from Mexico were increased 151,000 STRV, as discussed above. With total use unchanged, ending stocks are forecast to rise to 15.0 percent of use, compared with 12.9 percent in May.

The USDA forecasts total 2014/15 U.S. supply to increase by 811,000 STRV, with increases in beginning stocks and imports (Mexico) more than offsetting expected reduced cane sugar production. Beginning stocks, at 1.857 million STRV, are up 261,000 STRV. Total sugar production is lowered 140,000 STRV, due to lower sugarcane production in Florida and Louisiana based on processors' first projections for 2014/15. Total imports are forecast 690,000 STRV above May due to increased shipments from Mexico. With no changes in total use, ending stocks are forecast to rise to 15.8 percent of 2014/15 use from 9.1 percent.

Table 7 -- Mexico sugar supply and use, 2012/13 - 2013/14 and projected 2014/15, June 2014

Items	2012/13	2013/14	2014/15
1,000 metric tons, actual weight			
Beginning Stocks	966	1,460	818
Production	6,975	6,100	6,500
Imports	217	226	226
Imports for consumption	9	10	10
Imports for sugar-containing product exports (IMMEX) 1/	207	216	216
Total Supply	8,157	7,786	7,544
Disappearance			
Human consumption	4,287	4,306	4,306
For sugar-containing product exports (IMMEX)	384	384	384
Statistical adjustment	53	0	0
Total	4,724	4,690	4,690
Exports	1,973	2,278	1,907
Exports to the United States & Puerto Rico	1,818	1,708	1,337
Exports to other countries	155	570	570
Total Use	6,697	6,968	6,597
Ending Stocks	1,460	818	947
1,000 metric tons, raw value			
Beginning Stocks	1,024	1,548	867
Production	7,393	6,466	6,890
Imports	230	240	240
Imports for consumption	10	11	11
Imports for sugar-containing product exports (IMMEX)	220	229	229
Total Supply	8,646	8,254	7,997
Disappearance			
Human consumption	4,544	4,564	4,564
For sugar-containing product exports (IMMEX)	407	407	407
Statistical adjustment	56	0	0
Total	5,007	4,971	4,971
Exports	2,091	2,415	2,022
Exports to the United States & Puerto Rico	1,927	1,810	1,417
Exports to other countries	164	605	605
Total Use	7,099	7,387	6,993
Ending Stocks	1,548	867	1,004
Stocks-to-Human Cons. (percent)	34.1	19.0	22.0
Stocks-to-Use (percent)	21.8	11.7	14.4
High Fructose Corn Syrup (HFCS) Consumption (dry weight)	1,567	1,360	1,419

Source: USDA, WASDE and ERS, Sugar and Sweeteners Outlook; Conadesuca.
1/ IMMEX = Industria Manufacturera, Maquiladora y de Servicios de Exportación

Table 8 -- U.S. sugar: supply and use, by fiscal year (Oct./Sept.), June 2014.

Items	2012/13	2013/14	2013/14	2011/12	2012/13	2013/14
				1,000 metric tons, raw value		
Beginning stocks	1,979	2,158	1,857	1,796	1,958	1,685
Total production	8,981	8,490	8,355	8,148	7,702	7,580
Beet sugar	5,076	4,800	4,750	4,605	4,354	4,309
Cane sugar	3,905	3,690	3,605	3,543	3,348	3,270
Florida	1,867	1,760	1,770	1,694	1,597	1,606
Louisiana	1,686	1,600	1,520	1,530	1,451	1,379
Texas	173	140	135	157	127	122
Hawaii	179	190	180	163	172	163
Total imports	3,224	3,585	3,783	2,925	3,252	3,432
Tariff-rate quota imports	957	1,369	1,262	868	1,242	1,145
Other Program Imports	136	210	400	124	191	363
Non-program imports	2,131	2,006	2,121	1,933	1,820	1,924
Mexico	2,124	1,996	2,111	1,927	1,811	1,915
Total Supply	14,185	14,233	13,995	12,868	12,912	12,696
Total exports	274	325	250	249	295	227
Miscellaneous	-24	0	0	-22	0	0
Deliveries for domestic use	11,776	12,051	11,835	10,683	10,933	10,737
Transfer to sugar-containing products for exports under reexport program	80	100	100	73	91	91
Transfer to polyhydric alcohol, feed, other alcohol	32	35	35	29	32	32
Commodity Credit Corporation (CCC) sale for ethanol, other	153	316	0	139	287	0
Deliveries for domestic food and beverage use	11,511	11,600	11,700	10,442	10,523	10,614
Total Use	12,025	12,376	12,085	10,909	11,227	10,963
Ending stocks	2,160	1,857	1,910	1,959	1,685	1,732
Private	1,844	1,857	1,910	1,672	1,685	1,732
Commodity Credit Corporation (CCC)	316	0	0	287	0	0
Stocks-to-use ratio	17.96	15.01	15.80	17.96	15.01	15.80

Source: USDA, ERS, Sugar and Sweetener Outlook.

Table A-1 -- World sugar production, supply, and distribution

		2008/09	2009/10	2010/11	2011/12	2012/13	2013/14	2014/15
				1,000 metric tons, raw value				
North America								
Canada	Total Sugar Production	206	203	200	235	253	260	265
	Total Imports	61	70	94	130	130	95	95
	Total Supply	1,255	1,114	1,135	1,103	1,156	1,153	1,160
	Total Exports	1,522	1,387	1,429	1,468	1,539	1,508	1,520
	Total Use	93	37	89	83	46	33	35
	Ending Stocks	1,226	1,150	1,105	1,132	1,233	1,210	1,220
	Beginning Stocks	203	200	235	253	260	265	265
Mexico	Total Sugar Production	1,975	623	973	806	1,024	1,548	1,004
	Total Imports	5,260	5,115	5,495	5,351	7,393	6,731	6,890
	Total Supply	160	861	306	505	230	239	239
	Total Exports	7,395	6,599	6,774	6,662	8,647	8,518	8,133
	Total Use	1,378	751	1,557	985	2,090	2,543	2,158
	Ending Stocks	5,394	4,875	4,411	4,653	5,009	4,971	4,971
	Beginning Stocks	623	973	806	1,024	1,548	1,004	1,004
United States	Total Sugar Production	1,510	1,392	1,359	1,250	1,795	1,957	1,448
	Total Imports	6,833	7,224	7,104	7,700	8,148	7,693	7,706
	Total Supply	2,796	3,010	3,391	3,294	2,924	3,025	2,806
	Total Exports	11,139	11,626	11,854	12,244	12,867	12,675	11,960
	Total Use	123	192	225	244	249	295	227
	Ending Stocks	9,624	10,075	10,379	10,205	10,661	10,932	10,736
	Beginning Stocks	1,392	1,359	1,250	1,795	1,957	1,448	997
Total North America	Total Sugar Production	3,691	2,218	2,532	2,291	3,072	3,765	2,717
	Total Imports	12,154	12,409	12,693	13,181	15,671	14,519	14,691
	Total Supply	4,211	4,985	4,832	4,902	4,310	4,417	4,205
	Total Exports	20,056	19,612	20,057	20,374	23,053	22,701	21,613
	Total Use	1,594	980	1,871	1,312	2,385	2,871	2,420
	Ending Stocks	16,244	16,100	15,895	15,990	16,903	17,113	16,927
	Beginning Stocks	2,218	2,532	2,291	3,072	3,765	2,717	2,266
Caribbean								
Cuba	Total Sugar Production	135	102	114	59	109	149	150
	Total Imports	1,340	1,250	1,150	1,400	1,510	1,500	1,500
	Total Supply	23	0	0	0	0	0	0
	Total Exports	1,498	1,352	1,264	1,459	1,619	1,649	1,650
	Total Use	727	538	577	830	757	850	850
	Ending Stocks	669	700	628	520	713	649	650
	Beginning Stocks	102	114	59	109	149	150	150
Dominican Republic	Total Sugar Production	35	10	14	34	44	70	50
	Total Imports	510	520	510	553	556	575	600
	Total Supply	34	77	49	48	9	10	10
	Total Exports	579	607	573	635	609	655	660
	Total Use	239	261	204	211	165	215	218
	Ending Stocks	330	332	335	380	374	390	400
	Beginning Stocks	10	14	34	44	70	50	42
Other Caribbean	Beginning Stocks	132	121	108	99	96	96	92
	Total Sugar Production	189	168	187	182	178	190	210
	Total Imports	444	362	387	319	366	349	347
	Total Supply	765	651	682	600	640	635	649
	Total Exports	175	142	155	142	117	118	130
	Total Use	469	401	428	362	427	425	427
	Ending Stocks	121	108	99	96	96	92	92
Total Caribbean	Total Sugar Production	302	233	236	192	249	315	292
	Total Imports	2,039	1,938	1,847	2,135	2,244	2,265	2,310
	Total Supply	501	439	436	367	375	359	357
	Total Exports	2,842	2,610	2,519	2,694	2,868	2,939	2,959
	Total Use	1,141	941	936	1,183	1,039	1,183	1,198
	Ending Stocks	1,468	1,433	1,391	1,262	1,514	1,464	1,477
	Beginning Stocks	233	236	192	249	315	292	284

-- continued

Sugar and Sweeteners Outlook/SSS-M-310/June 18, 2014
Economic Research Service, USDA

		2008/09	2009/10	2010/11	2011/12	2012/13	2013/14	2014/15
				1,000 metric tons, raw value				
Central America								
Guatemala	Beginning Stocks	609	592	382	127	257	365	503
	Total Sugar Production	2,381	2,340	2,048	2,499	2,778	2,852	2,850
	Total Imports	0	0	0	0	0	0	0
	Total Supply	2,990	2,932	2,430	2,626	3,035	3,217	3,353
	Total Exports	1,654	1,815	1,544	1,619	1,911	1,950	1,950
	Total Use	744	735	759	750	759	764	768
	Ending Stocks	592	382	127	257	365	503	635
Other Central America	Beginning Stocks	440	436	507	493	545	606	619
	Total Sugar Production	2,071	2,194	2,128	2,462	2,719	2,700	2,792
	Total Imports	0	138	1	1	1	1	1
	Total Supply	2,511	2,768	2,636	2,956	3,265	3,307	3,412
	Total Exports	803	1,005	954	1,143	1,353	1,358	1,453
	Total Use	1,272	1,256	1,189	1,268	1,306	1,330	1,345
	Ending Stocks	436	507	493	545	606	619	614
Total Central America	Beginning Stocks	1,049	1,028	889	620	802	971	1,122
	Total Sugar Production	4,452	4,534	4,176	4,961	5,497	5,552	5,642
	Total Imports	0	138	1	1	1	1	1
	Total Supply	5,501	5,700	5,066	5,582	6,300	6,524	6,765
	Total Exports	2,457	2,820	2,498	2,762	3,264	3,308	3,403
	Total Use	2,016	1,991	1,948	2,018	2,065	2,094	2,113
	Ending Stocks	1,028	889	620	802	971	1,122	1,249
South America								
Brazil	Beginning Stocks	215	-1,135	-835	-285	-285	-535	-195
	Total Sugar Production	31,850	36,400	38,350	36,150	38,600	37,800	36,800
	Total Imports	0	0	0	0	0	0	0
	Total Supply	32,065	35,265	37,515	35,865	38,315	37,265	36,605
	Total Exports	21,550	24,300	25,800	24,650	27,650	26,200	25,250
	Total Use	11,650	11,800	12,000	11,500	11,200	11,260	11,355
	Ending Stocks	-1,135	-835	-285	-285	-535	-195	0
Colombia	Beginning Stocks	170	416	405	390	335	120	195
	Total Sugar Production	2,277	2,294	2,280	2,270	1,950	2,300	2,300
	Total Imports	139	185	160	322	332	330	330
	Total Supply	2,586	2,895	2,845	2,982	2,617	2,750	2,825
	Total Exports	585	870	830	876	542	580	600
	Total Use	1,585	1,620	1,625	1,771	1,955	1,975	1,995
	Ending Stocks	416	405	390	335	120	195	230
Argentina	Beginning Stocks	105	266	-22	81	232	444	141
	Total Sugar Production	2,420	2,230	2,030	2,150	2,300	1,780	2,000
	Total Imports	23	0	73	5	0	0	0
	Total Supply	2,548	2,496	2,081	2,236	2,532	2,224	2,141
	Total Exports	543	778	210	194	258	233	150
	Total Use	1,739	1,740	1,790	1,810	1,830	1,850	1,870
	Ending Stocks	266	-22	81	232	444	141	121
Other South America	Beginning Stocks	1,230	1,143	1,060	1,296	1,331	1,292	1,209
	Total Sugar Production	3,299	2,954	3,290	3,358	3,361	3,380	3,470
	Total Imports	1,487	1,644	1,872	1,668	1,732	1,604	1,586
	Total Supply	6,016	5,741	6,222	6,322	6,424	6,276	6,265
	Total Exports	351	377	359	309	364	406	347
	Total Use	4,522	4,304	4,567	4,682	4,768	4,661	4,737
	Ending Stocks	1,143	1,060	1,296	1,331	1,292	1,209	1,181
Total South America	Beginning Stocks	1,720	690	608	1,482	1,613	1,321	1,350
	Total Sugar Production	39,846	43,878	45,950	43,928	46,211	45,260	44,570
	Total Imports	1,649	1,829	2,105	1,995	2,064	1,934	1,916
	Total Supply	43,215	46,397	48,663	47,405	49,888	48,515	47,836
	Total Exports	23,029	26,325	27,199	26,029	28,814	27,419	26,347
	Total Use	19,496	19,464	19,982	19,763	19,753	19,746	19,957
	Ending Stocks	690	608	1,482	1,613	1,321	1,350	1,532

-- continued

		2008/09	2009/10	2010/11	2011/12	2012/13	2013/14	2014/15
					1,000 metric tons, raw value			
Europe								
European Union	Beginning Stocks	3,130	2,232	1,433	1,974	3,303	3,981	3,781
	Total Sugar Production	14,290	16,897	15,939	18,320	16,655	16,100	16,300
	Total Imports	3,180	2,561	3,755	3,552	3,935	3,500	3,750
	Total Supply	20,600	21,690	21,127	23,846	23,893	23,581	23,831
	Total Exports	1,332	2,647	1,113	2,343	1,662	1,500	1,500
	Total Use	17,036	17,610	18,040	18,200	18,250	18,300	18,500
	Ending Stocks	2,232	1,433	1,974	3,303	3,981	3,781	3,831
Other Europe	Beginning Stocks	471	362	319	306	292	317	319
	Total Sugar Production	629	719	737	732	689	684	684
	Total Imports	701	508	441	447	488	527	537
	Total Supply	1,801	1,589	1,497	1,485	1,469	1,528	1,540
	Total Exports	93	257	255	210	205	225	210
	Total Use	1,346	1,013	936	983	947	984	1,011
	Ending Stocks	362	319	306	292	317	319	319
Former Former Soviet Union 12								
Russia	Beginning Stocks	550	481	399	350	390	395	300
	Total Sugar Production	3,481	3,444	2,996	5,545	5,000	4,400	4,400
	Total Imports	2,150	2,223	2,510	510	735	1,150	1,100
	Total Supply	6,181	6,148	5,905	6,405	6,125	5,945	5,800
	Total Exports	200	34	17	300	15	30	50
	Total Use	5,500	5,715	5,538	5,715	5,715	5,615	5,510
	Ending Stocks	481	399	350	390	395	300	240
Other Former Soviet Union	Beginning Stocks	1,520	946	783	940	1,355	1,663	1,129
	Total Sugar Production	2,567	2,319	2,361	3,278	3,403	2,268	2,568
	Total Imports	1,581	2,040	2,024	1,349	1,590	1,889	2,067
	Total Supply	5,668	5,305	5,168	5,567	6,348	5,820	5,764
	Total Exports	652	759	696	877	905	832	796
	Total Use	4,070	3,763	3,532	3,335	3,780	3,859	3,815
	Ending Stocks	946	783	940	1,355	1,663	1,129	1,153
Total Former Soviet Union	Beginning Stocks	2,070	1,427	1,182	1,290	1,745	2,058	1,429
	Total Sugar Production	6,048	5,763	5,357	8,823	8,403	6,668	6,968
	Total Imports	3,731	4,263	4,534	1,859	2,325	3,039	3,167
	Total Supply	11,849	11,453	11,073	11,972	12,473	11,765	11,564
	Total Exports	852	793	713	1,177	920	862	846
	Total Use	9,570	9,478	9,070	9,050	9,495	9,474	9,325
	Ending Stocks	1,427	1,182	1,290	1,745	2,058	1,429	1,393
North Africa								
Egypt	Beginning Stocks	544	690	529	129	350	160	161
	Total Sugar Production	1,612	1,820	1,830	1,980	2,000	2,013	2,050
	Total Imports	1,382	978	1,120	1,480	1,050	1,208	1,220
	Total Supply	3,538	3,488	3,479	3,589	3,400	3,381	3,431
	Total Exports	100	330	550	389	400	350	350
	Total Use	2,748	2,629	2,800	2,850	2,840	2,870	2,910
	Ending Stocks	690	529	129	350	160	161	171
Other North Africa	Beginning Stocks	484	307	342	367	340	407	355
	Total Sugar Production	520	438	436	440	410	410	400
	Total Imports	2,628	2,505	2,636	3,230	3,659	3,185	3,290
	Total Supply	3,632	3,250	3,414	4,037	4,409	4,002	4,045
	Total Exports	112	161	406	347	567	503	505
	Total Use	3,213	2,747	2,641	3,350	3,435	3,144	3,185
	Ending Stocks	307	342	367	340	407	355	355
Total North Africa	Beginning Stocks	1,028	997	871	496	690	567	516
	Total Sugar Production	2,132	2,258	2,266	2,420	2,410	2,423	2,450
	Total Imports	4,010	3,483	3,756	4,710	4,709	4,393	4,510
	Total Supply	7,170	6,738	6,893	7,626	7,809	7,383	7,476
	Total Exports	212	491	956	736	967	853	855
	Total Use	5,961	5,376	5,441	6,200	6,275	6,014	6,095
	Ending Stocks	997	871	496	690	567	516	526

-- continued

		2008/09	2009/10	2010/11	2011/12	2012/13	2013/14	2014/15
				1,000 metric tons, raw value				
Sub-Saharan Africa								
South Africa	Beginning Stocks	227	79	100	158	162	189	469
	Total Sugar Production	2,350	2,265	1,985	1,897	2,020	2,425	2,500
	Total Imports	137	105	138	193	218	500	250
	Total Supply	2,714	2,449	2,223	2,248	2,400	3,114	3,219
	Total Exports	1,230	754	400	271	356	760	1,000
	Total Use	1,405	1,595	1,665	1,815	1,855	1,885	1,925
	Ending Stocks	79	100	158	162	189	469	294
Other Sub-Saharan Africa	Beginning Stocks	2,024	1,947	1,754	1,748	1,743	1,823	1,964
	Total Sugar Production	5,412	5,420	5,591	5,809	5,964	6,161	6,159
	Total Imports	4,272	5,048	5,278	5,228	5,879	6,170	6,230
	Total Supply	11,708	12,415	12,623	12,785	13,586	14,154	14,353
	Total Exports	1,647	1,284	1,309	1,423	1,591	1,612	1,618
	Total Use	8,114	9,377	9,566	9,619	10,172	10,578	10,750
	Ending Stocks	1,947	1,754	1,748	1,743	1,823	1,964	1,985
Total Sub-Saharan Africa	Beginning Stocks	2,251	2,026	1,854	1,906	1,905	2,012	2,433
	Total Sugar Production	7,762	7,685	7,576	7,706	7,984	8,586	8,659
	Total Imports	4,409	5,153	5,416	5,421	6,097	6,670	6,480
	Total Supply	14,422	14,864	14,846	15,033	15,986	17,268	17,572
	Total Exports	2,877	2,038	1,709	1,694	1,947	2,372	2,618
	Total Use	9,519	10,972	11,231	11,434	12,027	12,463	12,675
	Ending Stocks	2,026	1,854	1,906	1,905	2,012	2,433	2,279
Middle East								
Turkey	Beginning Stocks	405	505	549	462	355	157	103
	Total Sugar Production	2,100	2,530	2,274	2,262	2,130	2,300	2,300
	Total Imports	5	5	5	5	5	9	10
	Total Supply	2,510	3,040	2,828	2,729	2,490	2,466	2,413
	Total Exports	5	69	75	74	33	63	40
	Total Use	2,000	2,422	2,291	2,300	2,300	2,300	2,300
	Ending Stocks	505	549	462	355	157	103	73
Other Middle East	Beginning Stocks	2,696	1,464	1,514	1,601	1,576	1,636	1,573
	Total Sugar Production	819	1,342	1,106	1,186	1,180	1,130	1,130
	Total Imports	6,607	7,759	7,634	8,153	8,603	7,415	7,576
	Total Supply	10,122	10,565	10,254	10,940	11,359	10,181	10,279
	Total Exports	1,043	978	1,562	1,253	836	920	945
	Total Use	7,615	8,073	7,091	8,111	8,887	7,688	7,746
	Ending Stocks	1,464	1,514	1,601	1,576	1,636	1,573	1,588
Total Middle East	Beginning Stocks	3,101	1,969	2,063	2,063	1,931	1,793	1,676
	Total Sugar Production	2,919	3,872	3,380	3,448	3,310	3,430	3,430
	Total Imports	6,612	7,764	7,639	8,158	8,608	7,424	7,586
	Total Supply	12,632	13,605	13,082	13,669	13,849	12,647	12,692
	Total Exports	1,048	1,047	1,637	1,327	869	983	985
	Total Use	9,615	10,495	9,382	10,411	11,187	9,988	10,046
	Ending Stocks	1,969	2,063	2,063	1,931	1,793	1,676	1,661
South Asia								
India	Beginning Stocks	12,296	5,880	6,223	6,299	7,163	11,068	10,413
	Total Sugar Production	15,950	20,637	26,574	28,620	27,337	27,045	27,900
	Total Imports	1,358	2,431	455	188	1,722	100	0
	Total Supply	29,604	28,948	33,252	35,107	36,222	38,213	38,313
	Total Exports	224	225	3,903	3,764	154	1,800	1,500
	Total Use	23,500	22,500	23,050	24,180	25,000	26,000	27,000
	Ending Stocks	5,880	6,223	6,299	7,163	11,068	10,413	9,813
Pakistan	Beginning Stocks	1,163	550	830	1,470	1,350	859	1,134
	Total Sugar Production	3,512	3,420	3,920	4,520	5,000	5,215	4,860
	Total Imports	125	1,030	1,040	10	9	10	10
	Total Supply	4,800	5,000	5,790	6,000	6,359	6,084	6,004
	Total Exports	75	70	70	350	1,100	500	400
	Total Use	4,175	4,100	4,250	4,300	4,400	4,450	4,500
	Ending Stocks	550	830	1,470	1,350	859	1,134	*1,104*
Other South Asia	Beginning Stocks	865	632	570	564	572	591	611
	Total Sugar Production	290	255	295	265	290	290	190
	Total Imports	1,894	1,992	2,150	2,341	2,191	2,490	2,450
	Total Supply	3,049	2,879	3,015	3,170	3,053	3,371	3,251
	Total Exports	1	12	0	0	0	0	0
	Total Use	2,416	2,297	2,451	2,598	2,462	2,760	2,690
	Ending Stocks	632	570	564	572	591	611	561
Total South Asia	Beginning Stocks	14,324	7,062	7,623	8,333	9,085	12,518	12,158
	Total Sugar Production	19,752	24,312	30,789	33,405	32,627	32,550	32,950
	Total Imports	3,377	5,453	3,645	2,539	3,922	2,600	2,460
	Total Supply	37,453	36,827	42,057	44,277	45,634	47,668	47,568
	Total Exports	300	307	3,973	4,114	1,254	2,300	1,900
	Total Use	30,091	28,897	29,751	31,078	31,862	33,210	34,190
	Ending Stocks	7,062	7,623	8,333	9,085	12,518	12,158	11,478

-- continued

Table A-1 -- World sugar production, supply, and distribution

		2008/09	2009/10	2010/11	2011/12	2012/13	2013/14	2014/15
				1,000 metric tons, raw value				
East Asia								
Japan	Beginning Stocks	454	559	568	529	543	550	549
	Total Sugar Production	927	901	700	740	750	750	750
	Total Imports	1,279	1,199	1,331	1,230	1,330	1,365	1,390
	Total Supply	2,660	2,659	2,599	2,499	2,623	2,665	2,689
	Total Exports	1	1	1	1	1	1	1
	Total Use	2,100	2,090	2,069	1,955	2,072	2,115	2,138
	Ending Stocks	559	568	529	543	550	549	550
China	Beginning Stocks	3,965	3,784	2,355	1,621	4,140	6,793	8,494
	Total Sugar Production	13,317	11,429	11,199	12,341	14,001	14,346	13,700
	Total Imports	1,077	1,535	2,143	4,430	3,802	3,900	3,300
	Total Supply	18,359	16,748	15,697	18,392	21,943	25,039	25,494
	Total Exports	75	93	76	52	50	45	45
	Total Use	14,500	14,300	14,000	14,200	15,100	16,500	17,400
	Ending Stocks	3,784	2,355	1,621	4,140	6,793	8,494	8,049
Other East Asia	Beginning Stocks	554	644	619	664	653	689	692
	Total Sugar Production	65	70	70	70	65	65	65
	Total Imports	2,612	2,453	2,495	2,418	2,613	2,705	2,763
	Total Supply	3,231	3,167	3,184	3,152	3,331	3,459	3,520
	Total Exports	305	347	422	424	406	371	371
	Total Use	2,282	2,201	2,098	2,075	2,236	2,396	2,447
	Ending Stocks	644	619	664	653	689	692	702
Total East Asia	Beginning Stocks	4,973	4,987	3,542	2,814	5,336	8,032	9,735
	Total Sugar Production	14,309	12,400	11,969	13,151	14,816	15,161	14,515
	Total Imports	4,968	5,187	5,969	8,078	7,745	7,970	7,453
	Total Supply	24,250	22,574	21,480	24,043	27,897	31,163	31,703
	Total Exports	381	441	499	477	457	417	417
	Total Use	18,882	18,591	18,167	18,230	19,408	21,011	21,985
	Ending Stocks	4,987	3,542	2,814	5,336	8,032	9,735	9,301
Southeast Asia								
Thailand	Beginning Stocks	2,651	2,556	2,343	2,983	2,810	3,616	4,906
	Total Sugar Production	7,200	6,930	9,663	10,235	10,024	11,390	11,000
	Total Imports	0	7	19	0	0	0	0
	Total Supply	9,851	9,493	12,025	13,218	12,834	15,006	15,906
	Total Exports	5,295	4,930	6,642	7,898	6,693	7,500	8,300
	Total Use	2,000	2,220	2,400	2,510	2,525	2,600	2,700
	Ending Stocks	2,556	2,343	2,983	2,810	3,616	4,906	4,906
Philippines	Beginning Stocks	547	581	730	934	932	942	932
	Total Sugar Production	2,150	1,800	2,520	2,400	2,400	2,450	2,500
	Total Imports	23	250	41	30	35	40	45
	Total Supply	2,720	2,631	3,291	3,364	3,367	3,432	3,477
	Total Exports	239	101	507	282	275	300	300
	Total Use	1,900	1,800	1,850	2,150	2,150	2,200	2,250
	Ending Stocks	581	730	934	932	942	932	927
Other Southeast Asia	Beginning Stocks	1,215	880	1,312	1,254	1,064	1,634	2,021
	Total Sugar Production	3,218	3,060	3,183	3,403	4,075	4,125	4,275
	Total Imports	4,637	5,959	6,224	6,011	6,701	7,213	7,171
	Total Supply	9,070	9,899	10,719	10,668	11,840	12,972	13,467
	Total Exports	344	400	450	463	487	457	462
	Total Use	7,846	8,187	9,015	9,141	9,719	10,494	10,634
	Ending Stocks	880	1,312	1,254	1,064	1,634	2,021	2,371
Total Southeast Asia	Beginning Stocks	4,413	4,017	4,385	5,171	4,806	6,192	7,859
	Total Sugar Production	12,568	11,790	15,366	16,038	16,499	17,965	17,775
	Total Imports	4,660	6,216	6,284	6,041	6,736	7,253	7,216
	Total Supply	21,641	22,023	26,035	27,250	28,041	31,410	32,850
	Total Exports	5,878	5,431	7,599	8,643	7,455	8,257	9,062
	Total Use	11,746	12,207	13,265	13,801	14,394	15,294	15,584
	Ending Stocks	4,017	4,385	5,171	4,806	6,192	7,859	8,204

-- continued

		2008/09	2009/10	2010/11	2011/12	2012/13	2013/14	2014/15
				1,000 metric tons, raw value				
Oceania								
Australia	Beginning Stocks	400	487	413	193	64	83	65
	Total Sugar Production	4,814	4,700	3,700	3,683	4,250	4,300	4,400
	Total Imports	41	78	163	144	87	90	90
	Total Supply	5,255	5,265	4,276	4,020	4,401	4,473	4,555
	Total Exports	3,522	3,600	2,750	2,800	3,100	3,190	3,300
	Total Use	1,246	1,252	1,333	1,156	1,218	1,218	1,200
	Ending Stocks	487	413	193	64	83	65	55
Other Oceania	Beginning Stocks	157	104	82	77	56	53	63
	Total Sugar Production	300	213	195	235	220	240	245
	Total Imports	284	260	299	240	295	304	309
	Total Supply	741	577	576	552	571	597	617
	Total Exports	246	214	149	173	152	173	180
	Total Use	391	281	350	323	366	361	374
	Ending Stocks	104	82	77	56	53	63	63
Total Oceania	Beginning Stocks	557	591	495	270	120	136	128
	Total Sugar Production	5,114	4,913	3,895	3,918	4,470	4,540	4,645
	Total Imports	325	338	462	384	382	394	399
	Total Supply	5,996	5,842	4,852	4,572	4,972	5,070	5,172
	Total Exports	3,768	3,814	2,899	2,973	3,252	3,363	3,480
	Total Use	1,637	1,533	1,683	1,479	1,584	1,579	1,574
	Ending Stocks	591	495	270	120	136	128	118
World	Beginning Stocks	43,080	29,839	28,032	29,208	34,949	43,978	45,515
	Total Sugar Production	144,014	153,368	161,940	172,166	177,486	175,703	175,589
	Total Imports	42,334	48,317	49,275	48,454	51,697	50,481	50,037
	Total Supply	229,428	231,524	239,247	249,828	264,132	270,162	271,141
	Total Exports	44,962	48,332	53,857	54,980	54,490	55,913	55,241
	Total Use	154,627	155,160	156,182	159,899	165,664	168,734	171,459
	Ending Stocks	29,839	28,032	29,208	34,949	43,978	45,515	44,441

Source: USDA, FAS, PSD database.

Model: $Y = \alpha0 + \alpha1*[\text{annual trend}] + \beta1*OCT + \beta2*NOV + \ldots + \beta11*AUG + \varphi*[\text{Industrial Cane Deliveries}] + \psi\_i*[\text{Special Time Period effects\_i}]$
$\sum \Theta j* [\text{Direct Consumption Imports (DCI) from Mexico (j)}], j=0,1,2,3 : \text{monthly lag}$

		HFCS42		HFCS55		Industrial Beet Deliveries	
		Coeff.	t-Statistic	Coeff	t-Statistic	Coeff.	t-Statistic
Constant	α0	278,221	50.589	487,994	76.211	309,002	18.636
Annual Trend	α1	1,069	2.635	-5,989	-12.567	1,867	4.090
OCT	β1	---	---	---	---	---	---
NOV	β2	-24,499	-6.403	---	---	-30,100	-6.921
DEC	β3	-30,319	-7.913	---	---	-67,102	-13.669
JAN	β4	-17,667	-4.502	-19,448	-4.012	-22,781	-5.043
FEB	β5	-25,057	-6.386	-42,481	-9.001	-32,706	-6.633
MAR	β6	15,094	3.821	34,512	7.119	---	---
APR	β7	14,978	3.826	26,417	5.396	-14,257	-3.180
MAY	β8	27,817	7.060	65,626	13.315	---	---
JUN	β9	29,972	7.636	74,183	14.981	---	
JUL	β10	26,425	6.757	43,699	9.022	---	---
AUG	β11	39,436	10.070	70,191	14.517	15,273	3.362
IndustrialCane Deliveries φ		---	---	---	---	-0.319	-4.433
2009:10 - present	ψ1	-32,987	-8.951	---	---	---	---
2012:09 - present	ψ2	-25,960	-6.997	---	---	---	---
DCI (0)	Θ0	-0.275	-3.238	-0.062	-0.836	-0.168	-2.342
DCI(-1)	Θ1	-0.227	-2.655	-0.061	-2.042	---	---
DCI(-2)	Θ2	---	---	-0.060	-2.019	---	---
DCI(-3)	Θ3	---	---	-0.059	-0.795	---	---
Sum of DCI coefficients Θj				-0.242	-3.432		
(for polynominal distributed lag model - HFCS55 only)							
Adjusted R2		0.895		0.897		0.648	
Durbin-Watson		1.807		2.157		1.551	

Source: ERS, Sugar and Sweetener Outlook.

Contacts and Links

Contact Information
Stephen Haley, (202) 694-5247, shaley@ers.usda.gov (coordinator)
Verna Daniels, (202) 694-5301, vblake@ers.usda.gov (web publishing)

Subscription Information
Subscribe to ERS' e-mail notification service at http://www.ers.usda.gov/updates/ to receive timely notification of newsletter availability. Printed copies can be purchased from the USDA Order Desk by calling 1-800-363-2068 (specify the issue number).

Data

Tables from the *Sugar and Sweeteners Yearbook* are available in the Sugar and Sweeteners Topics at http://www.ers.usda.gov/topics/sugar/. They contain the latest data and historical information on the production, use, prices, imports, and exports of sugar and sweeteners.

Related Websites

Sugar and Sweeteners Outlook http://www.ers.usda.gov/Publications/SSS/
WASDE http://usda.mannlib.cornell.edu/MannUsda/viewDocumentInfo.do?documented=1194
Sugar Topics http://www.ers.usda.gov/topics/Sugar/

E-mail Notification

Readers of ERS outlook reports have two ways they can receive an e-mail notice about release of reports and associated data.

• Receive timely notification (soon after the report is posted on the web) via USDA's Economics, Statistics and Market Information System (which is housed at Cornell University's Mann Library). Go to http://usda.mannlib.cornell.edu/MannUsda/aboutEmailService.do and follow the instructions to receive e-mail notices about ERS, Agricultural Marketing Service, National Agricultural Statistics Service, and World Agricultural Outlook Board products.

• Receive weekly notification (on Friday afternoon) via the ERS website. Go to http://www.ers.usda.gov/Updates/ and follow the instructions to receive notices about ERS outlook reports, *Amber Waves* magazine, and other reports and data products on specific topics. ERS also offers RSS (really simple syndication) feeds for all ERS products. Go to http://www.ers.usda.gov/rss/ to get started.

www.ingramcontent.com/pod-product-compliance
Lightning Source LLC
Chambersburg PA
CBHW050409180526
45159CB00005B/2212